FACTS ABOUT SHERRY • HENRY VIZETELLY

C000156392

Publisher's Note

The book descriptions we ask book-sellers to display prominently warn that this is an historic book with numerous typos, missing text, images and indexes.

We scanned this book using character recognition software that includes an automated spell check. Our software is 99 percent accurate if the book is in good condition. However, we do understand that even one percent can be a very annoying number of typos! And sometimes all or part of a page is missing from our copy of a book. Or the paper may be so discolored from age that you can no longer read the type. Please accept our sincere apologies.

After we re-typeset and design a book, the page numbers change so the old index and table of contents no longer work. Therefore, we often remove them.

We would like to manually proof read and fix the typos and indexes, manually scan and add any illustrations, and track down another copy of the book to add any missing text. But our books sell so few copies, you would have to pay up to a thousand dollars for the book as a result.

Therefore, whenever possible, we let our customers download a free copy of the original typo-free scanned book. Simply enter the barcode number from the back cover of the paperback in the Free Book form at www.general-books. net. You may also qualify for a free trial membership in our book club to download up to four books for free. Simply enter the barcode number from the back cover onto the membership form on the same page. The book club entitles you to select from more than a million books at no additional charge. Simply enter the title or subject onto the search form to find the books.

If you have any questions, could you please be so kind as to consult our Frequently Asked Questions page at www. general-books.net/faqs.cfm? You are also welcome to contact us there.

General Books LLC™, Memphis, US/ 2012. ISBN: 9780217717588.

❧ ❧ ❧ ❧ ❧ ❧ ❧ ❧

rflHE controversy that had arisen with reference to Sherry--induced me in the autumn of last year to spend several months in those districts of the South of Spain whence our supply of this popular wine is derived, in order to ascertain the truth on the spot. During my sojourn I not only witnessed the vintaging of Sherry in many Jerez and San Lucar vineyards, but visited both vineyards and bodegas in the remainder of the extensive Sherry region; and while I profited by the facilities freely afforded to me wherever I went, I was especially careful not to limit my investigations merely to such matters as the growers and shippers of Sherry sought to commend to my attention. The result of what I saw and learned was published at the time in the columns of a well-known evening newspaper, and is now offered to the public in a revised and extended form. *Paris, October,* 1876. LIST OF ILLUSTRATIONS. PAGE.

Uniform in sice and price with the present work,

AND ILLUSTRATED WITH NUMEROUS APPROPRIATE ENGRAVINGS, CHAMPAGNES AND OTHER SPARKLING WINES.

By HENRY VIZETELLY, *Wine Juror for Q-reat Britain at the Henna Exhibition, Author of "The Wiuetofthe World Characterized and Clotted."*

COMPBISING

A Narrative of Personal Visits to the various localities where the most celebrated Sparkling Wines of the World are produced including descriptions of the cellars of the great Champagne manufacturers at Rheims and Epernay, of the Sparkling Wine establishments at Saumur and St. Peray, in the Jura, and the Cote d'Or, and along the Ehine, the

Main, and the Moselle. The work will also contain chapters on Neuchatcl Champagne, the miscellaneous effervescent Wines of Italy, Austria, Hungary, and Russia, and the Sparkling Catawba of the United States; together with a detailed classification of all the more important Champagne brands, the distinctive marks and labels of each manufacturer being arranged according to their respective ranks.

WARD, LOCK, AND TYLER, WARWICK HOUSE, PATERNOSTER ROW.

A few Copies only of the following Work remain on hand. *In crown 8to, 200 pages, ornamental cover, Is.; or cloth gilt,* Is. *6d.,* THE WINES OF THE WORLD CHARACTERIZED & CLASSED: WITH SOME PARTICULARS RESPECTING THE BEERS OF EUROPE.

BY HENKY VIZETELLY, *Chevalier of the Order of Franz-Josef. Wine Juror for Great Britain at the Vienna Exhibition of* 1878. NOTICES OF THE PRESS.

"Mr. Vizetelly discourses brightly and discriminatingly on crus and bouquets and the different European vineyards, most of which he has evidently visited. "—*The Times.* "A lively, brilliant', and exhaustive treatise on Wines."—*Daily News.*

"Written with the discrimination of a *gourmet* and the skill of a man of letters. Whether discoursing of the marrowy richness of unctuous red or the ambrosial perfume of pale yellow Hermitage, or enlarging on the bright limpidity of the maroon-coloured Cdte Kotie—a wine not to sip by itself but to drink with rich dishes and juicy viands—Mr. Vizetelly is equally at home." —*The Standard.* "One occasionally hears of critics who review books without having read them. No one can accuse Mr. Vizetelly of treating in similar fashion the Wines which he describes so well, and on which he passes such neat, and, as it seems to us, accurate judgments."—*Pall Mall Gazette.* "It reveals a large amount of knowledge on a subject which few not professionally interested in it study with so much care."—*The Globe.* "Mr. Henry Vizetelly on Wines and Beer deserves general attention."— *Saturday Review.* "Mr.

Vizetelly has collected in the two hundred closely-printed pages of his little volume much valuable information, and imparts it in a clear and intelligible manner."—*The Alhenatim.*

"A handy and entertaining little volume."—*The World.* "The book is a very charming one, and will tell the reader as much about the history of wines as he could gather from a whole library of vinous litersture."_2'A. *Graphic.* win' " critically follow and check off a fair portion of the Iwok, we -"-Lilian t/ Sf knowledge so far as that part is concerned, and we

""n,,? equally trustworthy, and, we may add, valuable."—*Court*

"The Wines of the World have inspired the pen of Mr. Henry Vizetelly, who combines the stylus of a prose Anacreon with the subtle palate of a *gourmet."—The Tablet.* "An admirable specimen of the work of an able writer who has thoroughly mastered his subject and can impart his stores of knowledge in the pleasantest way."—*Court Circular.* "Mr. Vizetelly's book will spread a vast amount of useful knowledge, and should store the mind of the budding judge of wiue with valuable hints and points and aphorisms respecting the various crus.'—*Llwjd's Newspaper.* "To this useful volume we may indeed most appropriately apply the term exhaustive."—*Sell's Weekly Messenger.* "Mr. Vizetelly's work forms a safe and intelligent guide upon the wine question. He has executed his task with impartiality, and stated the results of his inquiries with great skill and ability. We commend this cheap little volume to the attention of all who wish to acqunint themselves with the wonderfully varied vintages of the world."—*Public Opinion.*

"Since Cyrus Redding wrote his interesting work, nothing better hns appeared in English than the closely-printed shilling volume before us. It forms a pleasant book for the general reader, and is full of valuable information which the best-informed wine-merchant will be thankful to obtain. It is published, too, at a price so low that its cheapness is the only point likely to tell

against it, for the public will not easily believe that a shilling book can be more valuable than the heavy and expensive volumes on the same subject."— *Scotsman.* "Diners-out who profess to know a glass of wine would do well to make Mr. Henry Vizetelly's work their commonplace book, and thus astonish their friends with sallies of wit and wisdom. "—*Birmingham Daily Gazette.* "Mr. Henry Vizetelly is charmingly discursive on Wines."—*Leed Mercury.* "The extensive critical, analytical, and historical contents of the volume will be found exceedingly interesting and edifying to all interested in what is anything but a dry subject."—*Midland Counties Herald.* "The completeness of the particulars supplied, and the compactness and cheap price of the volume, mark it out as a hand-book for general use on the important subject of which it treats."—*Bristol Mercury.*

"Mr. Henry Vizetelly waxes poetic in his fluent work upon Wines."— *Birmingham Morning News.* "Ought to be in the hands of not only wine-merchants, but of every winebuyer."—*Leicester Daily Post.* "Mr. Henry Vizetelly has written charmingly of his subject, and his wealth of adjectives in finding pet *nuances* of expression is inexhaustible. There is not an unreadable page—we were almost going to say a dry one—in the whole liook. You fancy throughout you hear the ' glug-glug' of the wine. "—*Irish Times.* "The amount and quality of its information is extraordinary, and the writer is not biassed by favouritism to any country whose productions he describes and classifies."— *Cambridge Independent Press.* "Written by one who knows his subject thoroughly."—*Chester Courant.* "It is evident from passages scattered throughout his book that the author has become familiar with many of the finer vintages. at their scat of production in the principal wine-growing countries of Europe. What he imparts, therefore, is not second-hand information derived from former works on the same subject, and too often erroneous in their statements. but the result of personal experience and observation, aided by recognised judgment." —*Kentish Mercury.* WARD, LOCK, & TYLER, WARWICK HOUSE, PATERNOSTER ROW. THE AUTHOR OF FACTS ABOUT SHERRY,

Having occupied himself for some time past in collecting materials, is now engaged in writing

A HISTORY OF SHERRY.

and with the view of rendering the work as complete as possible, he invites communications from all who have a knowledge of, or take an interest in, the subject. He will feel much obliged to any one connected with the Sherry trade who will make the requisite researches and favour him with copies of the past-century business letters of interest referring to Sherry, of which numbers must be in the possession of old-established firms. Trilling and unimportant as these documents may seem, they will often help to complete some link and elucidate points that are obscure. Traditions and anecdotes bearing upon the history of noted shipping firms, and personal reminiscences of residents or sojourners at Jerez relating to the subject-matter of the propose 1 volume, will all be of value to the Author in the accomplishment of his task. Indeed, he invites hints and contributions of every description likely in any way to render his work complete and interesting.

The following are the contemplated subdivisions of the proposed volume:— of

FACTS ABOUT SHERRY.

I.—The Vintaging Of Manzanilla.

To Jerez by Way of Gibraltar—Shakspeare's Panegyric of Sherry—On Boartf the P. and O. Steamer "Australia"—The Sherry Capital and its Surrounding Vineyards—Excursion to San Lucur do Barrameda—Mr. R. Davies's Vineyard of Torre Breva—The Vintage there—Treading and Pressing the Grapes by Night—Vintagers at Supper.

In visiting the south of Spain in the early autumn no route is comparable to the Gibraltar one, which enables the tourist to avail himself of the admirable accommodation provided by the Peninsular and Oriental line of steamers. Less than five days on the open sea on board a floating hotel is immeasurably preferable to three or four days and nights in a stuffy railway carriage. In the former we find most of the comforts we have Ijeen habituated to on shore, and, what is of equal if not greater importance, one has not only complete confidence in the qualities of the ship, but in the nautical skill of its officers, all of whom pass a strict examination. The high pay, moreover, tempts into the service individuals of good social standing, so that the officers of the P. and O. have one

and all the courteous manners of gentlemen. People on board get rapidly acquainted, which adds materially to the pleasure of the passage. The ice is broken the first afternoon, and before the second sunset flirtations are already in full swing, so that mammas, on the whole, have rather an anxious time of it guarding their daughters from the attacks of " detrimentals"—subalterns about joining their regiments in India, or young fellows seeking their fortunes in Australia, to say nothing of trim-whiskered curates who, foregoing such pomps and vanities as linking, croquet, and kettledrums, are bent on converting the aboriginal heathen. The Cassandra-like warnings anent "Biscay's troubled waters" are likely to prove so many chimeras at this season of the year, and if only the same delightful weather is encountered as we luckily met with during the latter half of our passage, " so dulcet, delicious, and dreamy" will existence seem to the tourist, that he will quit the ship, as we left the "Australia" and her courteous commander, Captain Murray, with real regret. From Gibraltar it is only a few hours' sail to Cadiz, which rises in white-robed beauty out of the turquoise sea, while from Cadiz it is scarcely a few hours' rail to Jerez, the very heart of the sherry district, where from one year's end to another it is the habit to talk, think, and dream of little else besides wine, known in the mystical phraseology of the bodega as fino, palma, palo, cortado, raya, redondo, abocado, or basto.

Jerez enjoys the renown of having given its name to a wine which for upwards of three centuries has been famous with Englishmen, and is more or less celebrated all over the world. From Jerez (pronounced Herez) the transition to the sherris of the old English dramatists is obvious enough, and notably *to* the "excellent sherris" of Shakspeare, whose panegyric of a potation which, as he puts it, dries up all the foolish, dull, and cruddy vapours environing the brain, illumineth the face, and impels the heart to deeds of courage, will live as long as there are vineyards on the earth. The most remarkable features of the Andalusian frontier town are its vast bodegas, or wine-stores, girding it round like a rampart, its curious antique churches and its Morisco alcazar—half palace, half fortress—the residence of its former Moorish rulers. Its people are courteous—its señioritas types of southern *petite* grace and beauty. The town, too, has about it an unmistakable air of prosperous gentility; it is a model of cleanliness; and the dazzling whiteness of the houses, and the emerald brightness of their mouldings, rejas, and balconies, with the cool inner courts of the handsomer dwellings, set off with tropical plants and plashing fountains, combine, with the more or less gay and picturesque costumes of the common people, to give to the great sherry metropolis a cheerful and pleasing aspect. Its broader streets are planted with acacias or orange-trees, while its many little plazas, rendered gay with floral parterres, ornamented by stately palms, or bordered by umbrageous foliage, invite to the afternoon lounge or evening promenade.

The market-places of Jerez offer a series of bright pictures, which any artist with an eye for grouping and for brilliant contrasts of colour would delight in transferring to his sketchbook; while in the narrow winding thoroughfares of the more retired quarters of the town we constantly come upon little scenes of manners, in which portly shovel-hatted curas, stately senoras, and bright-eyed senoritas play a prominent part, and which seem to relegate one for the time being to the region of comedy and opera. For distraction the Jerezanos have, besides the customary carnival and spring and autumn fairs, their horse-races and bull-fights, their teatro, circo, and a couple of casinos, together with a roulette-table, at which a couple of grandees of this poor degenerate Spain act nightly as croupiers, handling the rake with the same seeming pride as their ancestors of old wielded lance and sword.

Vineyards encompass Jerez on all sides. Those scattered over the plain in the immediate vicinity of the town, more particularly on the north and

north-east (the soil of which is either sand or sand and clay impregnated with oxide of iron combined, and known as barro-arenoso), yield wine ordinarily of little repute; whereas the more distant plantations, covering the chalky slopes and ridges of the outlying amphitheatre of hills, the compact white soil of which is termed albariza, produce wines of the very highest character, and developing remarkable variety of flavour. Wine of an intermediate yet coarse quality comes from the vineyards of the lower slopes and valleys, the soil of which is dark earth, and goes under the name of bugeo.

In one corner of the sherry district proper is the little town of San Lucar de Barrameda, dating back to the dim traditional ages, and commanding the mouth of the Guadalquivir, which, judging by its flat monotonous banks hereabouts, scarcely merits the flowery praise bestowed upon it by the poets of all ages and nations. All the finer qualities of the pale, delicate, dry, tonicaltasting wine known as manzanilla, which we first came to hear of in England through Dr. Gorman's evidence before the Wine Duties Committee, and Mr. Eichard Ford's Handbook for Spain, come from the neighbourhood of San Lucar, where the vintage commences a fortnight earlier than at Jerez. Hither, therefore, I hied the day following my arrival, after first retracing my steps to Puerto de Santa Maria (Port St. Mary), which has its own vineyards and vast bodegas, and whence about a quarter of the sherry annually sent to England is shipped.

From Porto de Santa Maria one drove over to San Lucar in the conventional carretela, an antique style of vehicle, hung well upon its springs, but requiring four horses, with their customary ragged trappings and jingling bells, to drag it over the villainous pavements of the steep streets, and along the furrowed, sandy country roads. After passing some pleasant suburban gardens, with their tall flowering aloes and large-leaved tropical plants, we were soon among the few vineyards skirting the town, and, crossing a sandy heath stud-

ded with pines, emerged into the open country. A faint, ruddy-streaked purply haze of hills, indicating the finer Jerez vineyards, rose up on our right hand, while our road lay through fields of stubble eaten close down to the roots by browsing herds, or by brood mares turned out to feed after their task of threshing the lately-garnered corn had ended. We passed occasional huge-wheeled bullock-carts carrying empty wine-butts to San Lucar, and solitary pannierladen mules and donkeys; sighted ragged peasants tending thickly-fleeced sheep, or lazily watching herds of swine battening upon the skins of newly-trodden grapes, or drawing water from ancient wayside wells; occasionally startled an errant partridge or scattered a flock of staid-looking turkeys. The broad tracts of arable land, bounded by low hills, with some white farmhouse commonly crowning their summits, soon began to be intersected by patches of vineyards which, shut off by dusty hedges of prickly pear, broken here and there by a dilapidated gateway, eventually lined both sides of the road. A dark pine-grove rose on our left hand, and before us the white houses and bodegas of San Lucar, with their low-pitched roofs dominated by half-a-dozen church towers, spread themselves out in the midst of orangetrees, while the solid square keep of the Moorish castle frowned down disdainfully upon all. Beyond, the turquoise-tinted Guadalquivir flowed placidly on to the sea.

Troops of mules laden with panniers of dust-covered grapes, and occasionally carrying a couple of blue-shirted, crimsonsashed, hulking mulateros as well—for in this oppressive heat every beggar who gets the chance rides on horseback—are proceeding, enveloped in clouds of sand, to the different presshouses in the town; and as our vehicle rumbles along the irregularly-paved streets, bordered by the whitest of houses with the brightest of green shutters and balconies, we encounter files of donkeys carrying kegs and jars of water to thirsty souls sweltering in the surrounding vineyards. Heaps of grape-stalks, on which tawny-tinted, scantily-draped young urchins are sprawling, lie piled up in front of many an open gateway, through which glimpses are caught of casks and screw-presses, wooden shovels and pitchers, and capacious;troughs in which the grapes are trodden to a steady clockwork movement that would delight, if it did not absolutely frenzy, a Prussian drill-sergeant.

The most extensive vineyards at St. Lucar are those of Torre Breva, the property of the Due de Montpensier, but now rented by an Englishman, Mr. R. Davies, one of the large Jerez wineshippers. They are distant a long league from the town, and a drive bordered by fir-trees conducts through the plantations of vines to the house, distinguished by a tall square tower at one end. Here are no less than 320 acres of vines, not more than 200 of which, however, are bearing at present. Dotting the vineyards are groups of white outbuildings, and starting up in various directions are little huts of esparto, perohed upon four poles, and to which access is obtained bv aid of a short ladder. These are so many look-out places for the half-dozen guards, who, armed with old-fashioned Moorish firelocks, are employed to watch the vineyards from the commencement of July until the vintage is over, and are after the same fashion as corresponding structures encountered throughout the Medoc.

Upwards of 200 men were occupied with the vintage at Torre Breva. Advocates of women's rights will regret to hear that the labours of the softer sex are altogether dispensed with in the vineyards of the South of Spain. The men are broken up into gangs of ten, each with its separate capataz, and they certainly seemed to work with a will in a heat that rendered movement of any kind little short of heroic. They were a sturdy-looking, picturesque, raggedy lot, in broad sombreros, shirt-sleeves or linen jackets, and the inevitable scarlet or crimson sash wound tightly round their waists. Numbers of them came as far as sixty miles for a sixteen or seventeen days' hire, at 8 reals, or 20d., a day,

with onions for their soup, and a nightly shakedown on an estera in the casa de la gente of the vineyard. Some few dexterously plucked the bunches (the size and weight of many of which need to be seen to be credited) with their fingers, but the majority used a small bowie-knife—the lower class Spaniard's habitual companion and weapon of offence and defence—to detach the grapes. When the baskets, or the square wooden boxes known as tinetas, each holding about an arroba of grapes, weighing 25lb., were filled, the pickers hoisted them on their heads or shoulders, on which a small round straw knot was fixed for the purpose, and marched off in Indian file to the nearest almijar. Here the bunches were spread out in the sun to dry on circular mats of esparto, thus to remain for from one to three days, while all blighted fruit was thrown aside for conversion into either spirit or vinegar.

The sun by this time had well-nigh set, and preparations were made for pressing the grapes throughout the night, when, with a cooler temperature prevailing, there would be much less chance of precipitating the fermentation of the must. This pressing commenced between seven and eight o'clock, and was accomplished in a detached building under a low tiled roof, . but entirely open in front. Passing through the gateway, and stumbling in the dim light afforded by an occasional lamp fixed against the wall, over a rudely-paved courtyard, we found ourselves beside a row of large, stout wooden troughs, some 10 feet square and a couple of feet deep, raised about 3 feet from the ground, and known in the vernacular of the vineyards as lagares. The bottoms of these receptacles were already strewn with grapes lightly sprinkled over with yeso (gypsum), which, if spread over the whole of the bunches, would not have been greatly in excess of the amount of dust ordinarily gathered by a similar quantity of grapes conveyed in open baskets on the backs of mules from the vineyards to the pressing-places in the townsAt Torre Breva the sixty or more arrobas of grapes

(l,500lbs.) required to make each butt of wine were having from 211 is. to 41bs. of yeso sprinkled over them, or about half the quantity which would be used in a moist season. 1 was assured that at last year's vintage here not a single ounce of yeso was employed in the manufacture of upwards of 700 butts of wine. Of the supposed virtues and drawbacks of this employment of gypsum I shall speak by-and-by. Rising perpendicularly in the centre of each of the four lagares to a height of about seven feet is a tolerably powerful screw, which is only brought into requisition after the grapes have been thoroughly trodden. A couple of swarthy bare-legged pisadores leap into each lagar and commence spreading out the bunches with wooden shovels; and soon the whole eight of them, in their short drawers, blue-striped shirts, little caps, red sashes, and hob-nailed shoes, are dancing a more or less lively measure, ankle-deep in newly-crushed grapes. They dance in couples, one on each side of the screw, performing certain rapid pendulum-like movements which are supposed to have the virtue of expressing the juice more satisfactorily from the fruit than can be accomplished by mere mechanical means. Their saltatory evolutions ended, the trodden grapes are heaped up on one side and well patted about with the shovel, like so much newly-mixed mortar. This causes the expressed juice to flow out in a dingy brown turgid stream through the spout fixed in front of the lagar into a metal strainer, and thence into the vat placed beneath to receive it. Fresh grapes are now spread over the bottom of the lagar, and, after being duly danced upon, are shovelled on one side; and this kind of thing goes on until sufficient trodden murk has been accumulated to make what is called the pile.

The pisadores now retire in favour of the tiradores, or pressers, who, springing into the lagares, collect all the trodden grapes together and skilfully build them, by the aid of wooden shovels and that readier implement the hand, in a compact mass around the screw, just as an expert plasterer would build up a, circular column of compo. The form taken by this in the first instance, owing to the weight of the murk, is necessarily conical, consequently the base has to be neatly trimmed and the detached fragments built round the upper part of the column until this attains a height of some 5 ft. When perfected it is bound round with a long band of esparto, about 4 in. wide, from base to summit, and a flat wooden slab being placed on the top, with the nut of the screw immediately above it, the handles of the screw are rapidly turned, causing the juice to exude between the interstices of the esparto. For the first few minutes the labour is light enough. Presently, however, it becomes severe, and, although the pressers strain with all their might, they can only succeed in turning the nut by a series of successive jerks which necessitate the binding of their hands to the handle, for fear, when exerting their utmost strength, they should lose their hold of it, together with their footing on the slippery floor of the lagar, and so come to serious grief.

This treading and pressing of grapes goes on nightly for fourteen hours, with occasional intervals for refreshment, until the end of the vintage, lasting altogether for sixteen days. The pisadores are paid at the rate of 5 reals, about Is. , the fifty baskets, or arrobas, of grapes, enabling them to earn about 30 reals, or upwards of 6s., each per night. The tiradores receive *27* reals, or 5s. 6d., each for their night's work. Wine is freely given to them to encourage them to put forth all their strength, so as to get through the pressing of the grapes as speedily as possible. During a long night they commonly press at Torre Breva as many as sixty carretadas or cart-loads of grapes, which would ordinarily yield sixty butts of mosto, but on the occasion of our visit, through the excessive dryness of the season, gave much less than fifty.

After the stalks have been roughly stripped from the pressed grapes the skins are subjected to hydraulic pressure, but the must yielded by this means is invariably fermented by itself, and then commonly distilled into spirit, so

great is the dread which the cosechero of sherry has of tannin in his wine, although he knows it will impart keeping power, and that its harsh flavour passes off with time. Spirit is also distilled direct from the refuse grape-skins, which finally serve for manure. The must yielded by the first pressure of the grapes is poured through metal strainers into ordinary butts, and at Torre Breva these are forwarded by bullock-carts to San Lucar, where a municipal tax of a dollar and a half is levied on each. On their arrival at the bodega the contents, although fermentation may by this time have set in, are, in accordance with the prevailing San Lucar practice, at once transferred to other receptacles, the must of perhaps a dozen butts being divided equally among the same number of fresh casks.

Before returning to San Lucar we took a peep at the vintagers supping in the casa de la gente, a long, low, narrow, dimlylighted apartment, with a tiled floor, and a couple of huge bell-shaped depending chimneys, dividing it as it were into three. This is at once the refectory and dormitory for some 120 out of the 214 hands engaged in the vintage. Banged at equal distances down the centre of the apartment were a number of low tables, just sufficiently large to support a huge smoking bowl of bread and onion porridge of the circumference of a small sponging bath. Seated around each of these tables, with their eyes intently fixed on the steaming bowl, were seven ravenous men, who, quick as thought, plunged the wooden spoons with which they were armed first into the smoking porridge and next into heir distended jaws, taking special care never to make a false movement, and always to pile up their spoons as full as possible, until the once overflowing bowl was utterly void. The vintagers at Torre Breva managed to get through 360lbs. of bread daily, which had to be fetched from San Lucar, besides 6lbs. or 7lbs.. of grapes per head, equivalent in the whole to upwards of twelve butts of mosto. As, unlike Brillat-Savarin, they took their wine in the form of pills, none other was allowed them, and as

onion soup is not particularly provocative of garrulity, the meal passed off in comparative silence. Appetite appeased, the men puffed away at their cigarettes, and then proceeded to unroll the esteras hanging on their respective peg-s and stretch themselves full length upon them, soon to be overcome by sleep, which—with the thermometer at 90—wrapped them round about, as their compatriot Sancho Panza has it, like a warm cloak.

II.—The Bodegas Of San Lucar De Barrameda.

Wine-making at San Lucar—The Wine Bodega of the South of Spain—Seflor Hidalgo's Wines and Vineyards—Hanzanilla Soleras—Mode of Rearing the Wine—The Manzanilla Grape—Gipsy Concert at San Lucar.

Having seen manzanilla made in the vineyard I was anxious to ascertain whether any different mode of vinification was practised in the town, and, with that view, visited several of the pressing-houses in San Lucar de Barrameda, where, judging from the constant procession of mules with baskets of grapes from the surrounding vineyards which day after day threaded the narrow streets, a considerable quantity of wine was evidently being made. These mules are generally encumbered in regular Spanish fashion with more or less useless trappings, and if the whole of them are not adorned with bells the leading mule of the team will certainly be furnished with these jingling appendages. Not unfrequently, too, their flanks will be fantastically branded over with rude arabesques, indicative of their past or present gipsy ownership, and all of them will be duly muzzled with bands of esparto to check the poor brutes' well-known propensity for ripened grapes.

After being kept awake all night by the mosquitoes, which, as a rule, are prompt in acclimatising strangers, who discover to their cost the so-called mosquito-curtains to be a delusion, a mockery, and a snare, I started on my expedition shortly after the sun had risen, but that irrepressible luminary was already darting his fierce rays down the narrow side streets of San Lucar, rendering sweltering pedestrians like myself covetous of the little band of shadow to be found on the so-called shady side of the way. I was glad enough to dive into the cool courtyard indicated by my guide, where the pressing of grapes was going on under a low, slanting roof, supported on open arches, judiciously provided with large movable blinds of esparto to keep out the sun, and faced by a couple of shady acacias, which rose up majestically beside an old-fashioned well. As the mules ambled in with their panniers of grapes the latter were at once thrown into tubs or the neighbouring lagares, and then came the dancing upon them, followed by the building up of the pile and the straining away at the screw, precisely as at Torre Breva, excepting that the combined operations were performed by the same persons instead of by two distinct sets of men. Close by the measuring out of the expressed juice from the grapes was being accomplished by the aid of a metal measure perforated at the upper part to allow the must flowing through when it reached the point indicating half an arroba, with the view of ascertaining the amount of mosto yielded by grapes purchased from different vineyard proprietors, and who were to be paid at the rate of 30 reals, or 6s. 3d., per arroba—that is, a trifle over 2 gallons of must. When the vintage is prolific the price falls to 20 reals, just as it rises in years of scarcity like 1853, the epoch of the oidium, when manzanilla mosto commanded 100 reals the arroba, or about 6s. the gallon.

After visiting several pressing-houses we went over half a score of the principal bodegas at San Lucar, including those of Señores Hidalgo, Marin, Marquez, and Eodriguez, and Senoras Mergelina, de Otajola, and Manjon. The wine bodega in the south of Spain is not a cellar, but a lofty and capacious store, built on a level with the ground, and entered through a preliminary court or garden. It is commonly divided into from three to five aisles, is well lighted and ventilated, and has about it none of that pungent vinous odour pertaining to the close vaults in which wine is ordinarily stored. Moreover, the rays of the sun are carefully excluded from it by means of shutters or blinds of esparto. Some of these bodegas are sufficiently long to admit of one hundred butts of wine lying side by side in a single row. As the butts are commonly ranged in three, and occasionally four tiers, and as each aisle has casks stacked along either side of it, some conception may be formed of the vast number of butts of wine often housed in a single bodega. Señor Hidalgo, one of the principal growers of San Lucar and the largest holder of manzanillas, including the very finest qualities of this delicate aromatic wine, has, in addition to 1,000 butts of vino de color, usually stored in his bodegas no less than 5,000 butts of manzanilla divided into fifteen soleras in various stages of progressive development, from the pale, fresh-tasting, and remarkably fragrant young growths, to wines in their fifth and sixth year, and regarded in fine condition for drinking, including also a wine ten years of age, accorded a medal for progress at the Vienna Exhibition, with older wines which, although manzanillas, had developed much of the oloroso and amontillado characters belonging to the Jerez growths. The windows of his bodegas, which are placed rather high up, face the sea, to admit of a full current of cool sea air passing through the building when the wind blows from that quarter. Although this conduces materially to the evaporation of the wine, which, under ordinary circumstances, amounts to as much as 4 or more per cent. annually, Señor Hidalgo considers that any extra loss in this respect is amply compensated for by the marked improvement which the wine undergoes. Señor Hidalgo's wines are all the produce of his own vineyards, the most important of which, Miraflores la Baja, occupies some slopes a few miles distant from San Lucar, and yields 300 butts of manzanilla annually. Another vineyard in the same direction is La Punta del Aquila, while a third in the neighbourhood of Chipiona, a little seaside village lying between San Lucar and Rota, goes by the name of Santo Domingo.

At San Lucar, as at Jerez, the system of what are technically termed soleras—in other words, the building up of new wines on the foundation of older ones—prevails. As the older wines are drawn off to supply orders the deficiency created in the butts is made good by the addition of wine of the same character but a year younger, the place of which is supplied in a like manner by still younger wine, and this process is continued all down the scale. Manzanilla, it should be remarked, does not develop the endless variety of types which the finer wines of Jerez are known to assume, and, as a general rule, the wines in the San Lucar bodegas, although of the highest character, are not of the same great age as the richer, robuster, and more prized Jerez growths. With manzanilla ten years is about the extreme age of the bulk of the soleras, although their bases may date back for a century. The rearing of this wine appears to be as follows:—The mosto on being conveyed from the vineyard to the bodega is transferred, as already explained, into fresh casks, which, after being filled to within about a tenth of their full capacity, are ranged in rows one above the other, the lowest butts being placed on stone supports to prevent them from being attacked by a destructive insect common to these parts. In several bodegas we noticed that the bungs in front of the casks containing sweet wine were covered with tin as a protection against the San Lucar rats, which exhibit a strong partiality for vino duke, but leave ordinary wine untouched. During the period the must is fermenting—that is, until the ensuing February—the bungs are left entirely out of the casks, or placed loosely over the apertures, and in April the wine is racked from its lees, when it receives a moderate quantity of spirit, usually, we were repeatedly assured, no more than 1 or 2 per cent., and is then used to replenish the lowest scale of the solera. All the San Lucar almacenistas, or rearers of wine, of whom we made inquiries, were unanimous in stating that no further spirit was added to the wine up to the time it left their bodegas, when it would contain less than the orthodox 26 degrees of proof spirit. On the other hand, we were informed by the Jerez wine-shippers that much of the manzanilla when it reaches them indicates upwards of 26 degrees of strength.

Once or at most twice every year the wine is passed from the lower to the upper scales of the solera, which at San Lucar never number less than ten, when about half the contents of each particular butt is ordinarily left remaining in it. On these occasions the wine is always carefully selected, any casks which have undergone a disadvantageous change being put aside for blending with inferior qualities. This system of soleras necessitates the employment of a large capital, but it materially aids the development and improvement of the wine, the continual blending which it undergoes causing it to modify its harsher qualities.

Fine manzanilla up to its fourth or fifth year has a fragrant floral bouquet, which, combined with its singular freshness of flavour, causes it to assimilate in a remarkable degree to good Rhine wine. We tasted in different bodegas scores of wines ranging from their first up to their ninth or tenth years, and found that it was only when the wine was in its fourth or fifth year that the peculiar bitter aromatic flavour for which manzanilla is distinguished had completely manifested itself. In Senora Manjon's bodega we tasted manzanillas twenty years old. One of these wines had developed a distinct amontillado character, while another was of the nutty-flavoured oloroso type.

Manzanilla is the produce of the highly-prized species of grape which passes under the name of the listan in San Lucar, and is known throughout the Jerez district as the palomino bianco. The bunches are large, the berries being of a medium size, and when thoroughly ripe of a brownish golden tinge. Their flavour is pleasant, and they contain an abundance of saccharine. Much diversity of opinion prevails as to the origin of this name of manzanilla, the common belief being that it is owing to the San Lucar wine resembling the camomile (in Spanish manzanilla) in flavour; but persons likely to be well informed entertain no doubt that it takes its name from its striking similarity to a wine produced at a place called Manzanilla, some five-and-twenty miles from Seville. A hundred years ago the finer San Lucar growths used to be largely exported in jars to the Spanish South American colonies. To-day more than half the wine goes to Jerez and Puerto de Santa Maria for shipment, the remainder being consumed chiefly in the locality and at Cadiz and surrounding districts. The stocks of manzanilla, vino de color, and dulce, principally, of course, the former, at San Lucar, are estimated to amount ordinarily to 100,000 butts, an average vintage yielding about 18,000 butts.

Before quitting San Lucar we had an opportunity of witnessing a gipsy concert in the still-used cockpit of that pleasant little Andalusian town. The room was dimly lit up by a few feeble lamps, which gave scarcely more light than the moon itself shining through the open window. The performers, three men and a woman, the latter in a light muslin gown, were posted in the pit itself. The audience, with occasional exceptions, belonged to the gipsy race, and the appearance among them of a trio of Englishmen caused considerable sensation, and even led to the reinforcement of the few municipal guards told off to preserve the peace at the entertainment. The singing of the men was highly characteristic, and very much after the Arab style. A few words in a half-Spanish, half-Gitano dialect, sung in a high-pitched and somewhat melancholy key, were succeeded by a pause filled up by some weird notes of the guitar, the audience keeping time by loudly clapping their hands, and indulging in frenzied acclamations of delight whenever any favourite passage caught the ear. The singing was varied from time to time by the woman dancing one of those slow, languid, semi-voluptuous movements common in the East, with the guitar accompanying each successive motion of her flexible frame.

IH.—Jerez Vineyards North Op The Town.

The Amoroso, Romano, la Paz, and Ducha Vineyards of Senor Gonzalez— The Abandoned Oratory—Potluck with the Vintagers—The Vineyard of Sefior Jose' Pemartin in the Cerro de Santiago—Proceedings of a Jerez Mob in 1871—Sefior Domecq's Majuelo at High Macharnudo—The "Alumbra"— Senor Domecq's System of Vinification—View from the Tower at High Macharnudo—The Press-house, Bodega, and Casa de la Gente— The Almocaden and A. B. Vineyards.

The Jerez vineyards—upwards of fifteen thousand acres in extent—are distributed over a tract of undulating country some twelve and a half miles long by less than ten miles broad, the town standing nearly in the centre. The first vineyards we visited belonged to Sefior Gonzalez, and were distant from one to two leagues of Jerez in a northerly direction. In the outskirts of the town we passed the deserted palatial chateau, surrounded by large and beautiful gardens, the construction of which some dozen years ago simply ruined one of the richest sherry shippers of Jerez. A grove of olive-trees occupied the slope on our left hand; and this passed, our vehicle went ploughing a foot deep through a primitive sandy road, skirted by tall banks and hedges of prickly pear—dark cypress-trees in couples flanking the large gateways which conduct along shady avenues to pleasant villas among the vines. Soon we came into an open plain covered with scanty stubble, which, after having been eaten almost bare by oxen, was considerately given up to herds of goats. The Gibalbin mountain rose up some leagues ahead of us, and the more distant ranges of the Sierra de Jerez, including the loftier peaks of the Pefion de San Cristobal, las Cabras, and el Algibe, bounded the horizon on the right hand, while undulating hills, planted with vines and with handsome country-houses crowning their summits, shut in the view upon the left. After a time wo dipped down into a hollow and followed a level road, skirted on one side by vineyards dotted over with groups of men gathering grapes or marching in gangs with their piled-up tinetaa deftly balanced on their heads, to spread out the bunches to dry in the neighbouring almijar. An occasional inscription on some gateway or along the facade of a casa de vina intimated that one or the other patch of vines was named after our Lady of Consolation, our Lady of the Angels, or a favourite patron saint. Sweeping sharply round to the left and ascending a low hill, we arrived at the casa of the Amoroso vineyard, surmounted by a fantastical weathercock formed of the painted figure of a vintager plucking grapes. Here we found several of the primitive mulecarts common to the south of Spain being laden with butts of mosto for Jerez. The casks, after having their hoops tightened by the cooper, were mounted on to the carts, when the bungs were withdrawn and zigzag-shaped metal tubes were inserted in their place, to allow the carbonic acid generated in the fermenting mosto to escape, and prevent the mosto itself running over from the excessive jolting of the butts along rough country roads, or the violence of the fermentation induaed by exposure to a temperature only a little below 100 deg. Fahrenheit.

The Amoroso vineyard, in the famous viticultural district of Carrascal, is about sixty acres in extent, and contains principally vines of the prized palomino species, planted only a little more than four feet apart. Most of the vines range from fifty to sixty years old, which conduces materially to the high quality of the wine, fine wine, as a rule, being rarely produced from vines which have not attained or passed their prime. The aspect of the Amoroso vineyard is westerly, so that it enjoys the advantage of escaping the scorching blasts of the dreaded Levanter. In the press-house, containing half-a-dozen lagares, furnished with the old-fashioned wooden screw, the grapes were being trodden and pressed in the manner we have already described, and which is universal throughout the sherry district. Owing to the excessive dryness of the season, the same small quantity of gypsum was being used as we saw employed at San Lucar.

From the Amoroso vineyard it is only a short drive to that of Romano, some sixty-five acres in extent, and occupying a neighbouring slope in the same district of Carrascal. Here we found nearly a dozen different species of vines intermingled, including black as well as white varieties. The vintage here, as in all the vineyards around Jerez, would last scarcely two-thirds of the ordinary time, owing to a general deficiency in the crop, which in many vineyards fell short of even half of an average one.

On leaving Romano the horses' heads were turned northwards, and onward we went for several miles in a straight line, across lightly-ploughed uninclosed fields, to the most distant of the Jerez vineyards. On the neighbouring hills numerous brood mares and their foals were huddled together to obtain all the shade they could from the fierce rays of the noonday sun. We noticed that they invariably posted themselves on the brow of the hill, and on the side facing the wind, so as to secure the full benefit of the faintest breeze. There were olives to the right and olives to the left of us, with a large farm on the skirts of the plain. Presently we struck a narrow road, and five minutes afterwards were driving through the Vina de la Paz—the Vineyard of Peace—and up to its little white-walled casa, set off with bright green shutters and balconies. Near the large oldfashioned well in front, some vintagers, in the midst of a plague of wasps, were spreading out newly-gathered grapes, principally of the palomino and mantuo varieties, on round mats of esparto, there to dry in the full blaze of a southern sun. The roof of the adjacent press-house, where the pisadores, or treaders, and the tiradores, or pressers, were steadily at work, was much loftier than usual, and a full current of air swept through the building, one great advantage of which was the retarding of any too hasty fermentation of the must.

A walk through the vines, kept according to custom scrupulously free from weeds, brought us to the neighbouring vineyard of Ducha, upwards of eighty acres in extent. Here, although the crop was small, the grapes were remarkably fine. They were being trodden in a lagar by three men abreast—all with their eyes steadily fixed upon their work as though determined that not a grape should escape their heavy tread. The must yielded by them was clearer than usual, and remarkably sweet. The daughter of the capataz of the vineyard, a charming little Spanish girl in light striped dress and nankeen apron, followed us about everywhere, gravely watching our movements with folded arms and inquisitive eyes. At one end of the casa she pointed out to us a little oratory with a covered altar inclosing a painting of the Virgin and Child, the green-and-gold doors of which were decorated with religious emblems. In more pious times a little bell above the roof used to summon the vintagers for some distance around to Sunday mass. Of late years, however, the religious sentiments of the Andalusian peasant have sensibly declined under the influence of revolutionary teaching, and the little Ducha oratory, like scores of similar ones around Jerez, is no longer applied to its intended purpose. The capataz of the vineyard had, nevertheless, turned it to advantageous account, for from the rafters of the roof hundreds of huge bunches of selected grapes hung suspended to long canes, with the object of preserving them for table use until as late a period of the year as possible.

The court in front of the casa de la vina was planted round with the adelfa, or rose laurel, a favourite shrub in the Jerez vineyards, and still in all the magnificence of its bloom at this season of the year. Two stately cypresses stood as sentinels at the entrance to the vineyard, on the highest point of which another of these funereal trees was planted. Prom hence a most extensive view was obtained over the broad plain, covered in many parts with dwarf palms, as well as over the neighbouring olive-groves and the hill-slopes planted with vines, while rising up grandly behind all were the tall peaks of the distant Sierra— grey, sombre, and cold in the surrounding flood of sunlight.

Hot as the day was, our long drive and the exhilarating atmosphere had so far sharpened our appetites that we were glad to accept an invitation to share potluck with the Ducha vintagers, whose dinner-hour it chanced to be, and better potluck it was never our fortune to fall in with. It consisted of a ragout of mutton, stewed in olive oil and flavoured with capers and sweet capsicums, and was tender as a spring chicken. It was necessary to handle one's knife deftly, for forks are looked upon as super

Unities in these parts. When dinner was over the men betook themselves to the stone benches beneath the arcade of the casa and silently smoked their cigarettes. The Andalusians enjoy the reputation of being light-hearted and gay, but in the vineyards their light-heartedness seems to subside into taciturnity, and their gaiety to partake of the lugubrious.

One of the most important viticultural districts around Jerez, both as regards the quality of its products and the extent of its vineyard area, is that of Macharnudo; and the renowned Majuelo, belonging to Sefior Domecq, is at once the largest and most celebrated vineyard of the locality. "Majuelo" really means a young plantation of vines; and this fine old vineyard, planted in part upwards of eighty years ago by the founder of the oldest existing firm in Jerez, still retains its juvenile name. It lies north-west of the town; and to reach it we drive along the usual sandy road, past the customary olive-grove in the outskirts, between the interminable prickly pear hedges, and through vast uninclosed fields of stubble, meeting seemingly the same lumbering bullock-carts with their jolting butts of mosto, the same jaunty redsashed caballeros astride their ambling mules, the same patiently-enduring donkeys, and the same half-fed herds of goats and oxen. We turned out of our way to visit the Cerro de Santiago, and took the opportunity of inspecting the vineyard belonging to Sefior Jose Pemartin, who has a fine house with a tower perched upon the summit of the hill.

During the troublous times of 1871 a Jerez mob collected here and sent out scouts to Trebujena and elsewhere for reinforcements before making a contemplated attack upon the sherry capital. To pass away the time they broke into the wine-cellars and swallowed their contents; then, after setting fire to the house, valiantly decamped. The surrounding vineyard is some seventy acres in extent, and the vines are, as usual, mainly of the palomino and the Pedro Jimenez varieties. As it was late in the season when we made our visit we found the vintage just concluded, and the mosto stored according to the practice prevailing at this vineyard in the bodega belonging to the casa, in preference to exposing it to a tropical temperature by carting it to Jerez. The result would seem to justify this course, for the wine invariably turns out well.

We now drove to High Macharnudo, to the vineyard of Senor Domecq. Here the vintage was also finished, and about a thousand men were engaged on what is termed the alumbra— that is, loosening the soil and forming a square trough round the stem of each vine, to enable it to secure the full benefit of the autumn rains. This operation would occupy a fortnight, and as the vineyard is 500 acres in extent, each man would get through his quarter of an acre (or trough round about 450 vines) in a week, for which he would receive 54 reals, nearly 12s. The total annual cost per acre of a Jerez vineyard varies from £10 to as much as.£18 in certain instances. The labour done will include, in addition to the vintaging of the crop, the various prunings of the vines, the placing of supports to sustain the heavier bunches of grapes, the several operations of loosening and turning over the soil, weeding it, troughing round the vines, and the subsequent filling up of the holes. The vineyards are never manured excepting in the case of newly-planted vines. Over some fifty acres or more of Senor Domecq's vineyard the vines are not in full bearing; some are very old, while others, planted to renew those that have died off, have not yet arrived at maturity. Here, as in all the good vine-

yards, the palomino variety of grape predominates. When the vines are pruned one braneh is left with a single knot and a second branch with four or five knots upon it. Senor Domecq has found by experience that the best wine is produced by mixing the bunch of grapes from the branch with the single knot (the juice of which is very sweet) with the central bunches of the other branch, the berries of which, as a rule, are smaller than the rest, have thick skins, and consequently contain an abundance of tannin. The wine thus produced is of high character, and remarkable for fulness and strength. The result of the vintage just concluded gave only 450 butts, of which 385 were fine dry wine, and the remainder Pedro Jimenez and Tintilla—the latter from sweet black Alicante grapes after they had been exposed to the sun for a considerable time. This wine, unlike the Eota Tent, is perfectly fermented, the mosto being left upon the skins for fourand-twenty hours, and then drawn off to complete its fermentation in other casks.

A large inconvenient residence, dominated by a lofty square tower and partly hidden by a belt of ornamental trees, occupies the most elevated point of High Macharnudo. A winding avenue of acacias, mulberry-trees, and cypresses leads to the house, the principal apartments of which, long since unoccupied, are decorated in a fantastic fashion, and recall the time of the First French Empire, when Joseph sat on the Spanish throne and Soult lorded it in Andalusia. The view from the tower embraces a perfect panorama of vine-clad slopes and hills, scattered farms, white-walled towns, and hazy mountain peaks. The adjacent press-house—the largest we have ever seen—contains as many as twenty lagares. Adjoining is a capacious bodega capable of storing 1,000 butts, but the mosto is no longer left to ferment there. The principal casa de la gente is a vast apartment of three aisles, and accommodates several hundred men, for the daily ragout of whom and their fellows about fifteen sheep were being regularly killed.

In face of High Macharnudo and on the opposite side of the Trebujena road are the Almocaden vineyards, whose Moorish name, signifying captain of troops guarding the camps, suggests a somewhat remote antiquity. The wine produced here, and especially in the vineyard of Matamoros, is highly valued at Jerez. Another excellent vineyard, known as the A. B.—these being the initials of a former proprietor—adjoins Senor Domecq's Majuelo on the other side. It is only thirty acres in extent, but it produces an admirable fino wine of remarkable delicacy, which the owner, Senor Gonzalez, rears and ships intact. A few hundred yards off is another small vineyard belonging to the same proprietor, which also yields a high-class wine, though not of the same refined character.

TV.—Othee Jeeez Vineyards.

The Cerro de Obregon Vineyard of Messrs. Cosens and Co.—Treatment of the Grapes for Vino Dulce—The Arrangement of the Casa de la Vina—Wasted Raisins—Breakfast at the Vineyard—Sequestrations by Brigands in the Neighbourhood of Jerez—The Successful Resistance of Aunt Matias's Nephew—Short Shrift to Captured Brigands—The San Julian, Leon, and Las Canas Vineyards—Bobbery of the Guard at the latter—The Tula Vineyard, with its mock Moorish Castle and Battlemented Alraijar—Vineyards of the Plain—The Vineyard facing the Spoon Wineshop—SeSor Campo's Vineyard—Waste of Labour in working both Wine-Press and Plough— The Cartnja Monastery and its Ancient Bodega.

A Short league to the west of Jerez, and along the San Lucar road, is the Cerro de Obregon vineyard, belonging to the large shipping house of Cosens and Co. Like the vineyards of Carrascal and Ducha already described, the soil is albariza, and, although the vines are scarcely twenty years old, the wine yielded is of fine quality. We started off there early in the morning, our way lying through undulating country covered with stunted stubble, of which herds of oxen were having the run in search of such stray wisps of straw as might hith-

erto have escaped their observation. Mule and bullock carts, jolting along to Jerez with butts of mosto, and raising dense clouds of dust in their wake, continually met us on the road, in company with much-enduring donkeys, happy enough when their ordinary load was not supplemented by a couple of strapping fellows astride their unwilling backs.

The vineyard, upwards of eighty acres in extent, and over which not so much as a single weed or a blade of grass could be detected, covers the sides of a steep hill, having on its summit a small plateau, where the casa de la vina has been erected. Hence a beautiful and extensive view is obtained over farms and a succession of rolling ground, rich vine-clad hills, slopes, and ridges, intersected bv winding roads, and dotted over with bright-looking little white casus hemmed in by occasional trees, and with scores of look-out perches of esparto; for far and near around Jerez watch has to be kept over the grapes from the moment they begin to ripen until the vintage is concluded. To the left, in the mid-distance, we could discern the church-towers and bodegas of Jerez, flanked by a long sweep of purple hills fading away in the hazy sunshine, while on the far-off horizon a glimpse was obtained of the Bay of Cadiz and of the masts of the shipping there riding at anchor.

At the moment of our arrival gangs of men from different parts of the vineyard kept coming to the almijar, or large walled court in front of the casa, with richly-bronzed grapes piled up in their little square wooden tinetas, tapering towards their base, and provided with flexible handles of esparto. As vino dulce was being made, the grapes, which were at once spread out, had to remain exposed to the sun for several days. Some neighbouring groups were engaged in detaching those grapes already sufficiently dried from the larger stalks preparatory to their being trodden and pressed in the numerous lagares, where pisadores and tiradores were actively at work.

The casa de la vina of the Cerro de

Obregon is a good type of the kind of building commonly found throughout the Jerez vineyards. It consists of merely a single story, and its walls, pierced with only a few small windows, are of dazzling whiteness. The central portion of its front is occupied by the customary shady arcade, with bright flowering plants trained up its solid square pillars, the rooms of the capataz and his family being situated on the right; while the stabling and the quaint-looking kitchen, with its collection of huge copper caldrons belonging to the casa de la gente, where the men employed in the vineyard are accommodated, occupy the wing on the left. In the rear is the casa de la gente itself, and in a line with it and running behind the apartments of the capataz is a capacious bodega for storing the mosto until it is conveyed on mule or bullock carts to Jerez. At the back of the building is a long press-house containing as many as nine lagares, besides the usual hydraulic press, where the several processes of treading the grapes, building the pile, jerking the screw, and pumping up the hydraulic press were going on at the same time.

We noticed here that, although sweet wine was being made, a large percentage of grapes which had dried on the vines till they had become complete raisins, and which nevertheless could have been made to yield a considerable amount of concentrated juice, usually escaped pressure. That they should do so in the lagares was a matter of no surprise, and it seems that, owing to their becoming embedded among the pressed skins of the general mass of grapes, even the hydraulic press was powerless to crush them. Among them, no doubt, were a certain number of *uvas muertas,* or dead shrivelled grapes; still in some vineyards we had observed hundredweights of perfectly good raisins—from which, at Chateau d'Yquem, the wine known as the *creme de tSte* is produced—scarcely one with its skin broken, but which had been thrown aside with the refuse to be exchanged with the neighbouring farmers for straw and be given by them to their pigs, who doubtless duly appreciated the sacchariferous delicacy.

After inspecting the vintagers at their early dinner in the dimly-lighted, cool casa de la genta, we were about proceeding to another vineyard when a lad trotted up on a mule with wellladen panniers swung over its sides. We learned with satisfaction from one of the proprietors of the Cerro de Obregon, who was doing the honours of the vineyard, that these contained our breakfasts, which comprised prawns the size of infant lobsters, red mullet fresh that morning from San Lucar, succulent Spanish ham, and cutlets, with various etceteras, among which was a dish composed of new-laid eggs and finely-chopped tomatoes, fried together in oil at the casa, and forming a kind of paste capable of sending the most fastidious Parisian gourmet into raptures, and giving even a finer flavour to our host's choice old amontillado.

Remarking during breakfast upon the beautiful view which the site occupied by the casa de la vifia commanded, we asked our host why, the spot being so convenient to Jerez, and the air among the vine-clad hills so delicious, he did not build a villa there. "Because," he replied, " I might incur the risk of being sequestrated." On asking for an explanation he informed me that a person of any means could scarcely live even that short distance from Jerez without the chance of himself or some member of his family being carried off to the mountains, only to be released on payment of an exorbitant ransom. "True," said he, " during vintage-time certain families still occupy their country-houses among the vines, as was the general custom some years ago, when the vintage furnished the occasion for a round of visits and festivities; but they only do so," continued he, "with arms constantly within reach, or at considerable risk. " Calling his manager, he asked him to give the particulars of some sequestrations of recent date. From him we learned that a couple of months ago the son of a farmer near Arcos, distant five leagues from Jerez, was carried off and kept for more than a fortnight in the mountains, and only eventually released

on his father's paying a certain ransom. So recently, too, as last month the nephew of an old lady, known in her neighbourhood as " Aunt Matias," was carried off from a place called Paterna, also five leagues from Jerez. The young fellow lived with his aunt on a small farm, and, as she was unable to scrape together the thousand dollars or so demanded as ransom, his captors set him at liberty on receiving' one-third of that sum and being promised the remainder in two equal portions at stated intervals. The first instalment was paid promptly enough, but not the final one, whereupon a couple of brigands made their appearance; and not succeeding in meeting with the man they were in quest of, rather than return and report the utter failure of their mission to their comrades, they decided upon carrying off a cousin of their former prisoner as a sort of hostage. Just, however, as they were about pouncing upon their prey a blacksmith's assistant inconveniently appeared upon the scene, and one of the brigands had ingeniously to draw him aside, while his comrade, by the menace of a loaded gun, obliged Aunt Matias's second nephew to accompany him. As soon as they reached a retired spot the brigand commanded his prisoner to ʃ halt, that he might bind his arms, according to custom, behind his back. The left arm was first secured, and as the brigand was preparing to bind the right one, his victim, glancing over his shoulder, perceived that his captor had laid down his gun some little distance off. Quick as thought he drew a long knife from his sash and made a stab at the brigand, but the knife having stuck fast in its sheath, merely dealt a stout blow, though fortunately sufficient to stagger the ruffian. Before the latter could recover himself and seize his gun the nephew of Aunt Matias clenched the sheath between his teeth, and, swiftly drawing out the knife, stabbed the brigand mortally. Ere the scoundrel died he called upon his comrade by name for help; but by the time the latter came up their prisoner was beyond reach of the shots fired after him. The brigand, after giving useless chase, returned and

calmly mutilated the face of his dead companion in order that he might not be recognised. Aunt Matias's nephew, however, remembered the name that the dying man had called out, and this led to its owner being captured by the authorities with several others of the band. At that moment they were believed to be in prison at Seville awaiting trial, still it is not unlikely they were already shot. In Spain it is a common practice to shoot prisoners of their class, and by official order, while conducting them from one place of imprisonment to another, on the pretence that they have either mutinied against their guards or made an attempt to escape. Some political prisoners who heard the ominous order given, "Take especial care your prisoners do not escape," and knew that it meant "Kill them on the road," at once asked leave to have their hands and feet shackled, that their guards might have no excuse for shooting them down in cold blood.

The brigands who make occasional descents in the more immediate vicinity of the sherry metropolis are not, it would appear, devoid of all feelings of humanity, for a Jerez gentleman sequestrated by them a few years ago was considerately provided with white bread daily, and duly prayed with at night during his enforced sojourn among the bracing air of the Sierra. He was none the less pleased, however, when his ransom of 8,000 dollars in specie arrived and he was permitted to bid his courteous captors an affectionate adieu.

On quitting the Cerro de Obregon we proceeded on foot to the adjacent vineyards of San Julian, comprising some 350 acres of excellent chalky soil, planted principally with the palomino variety of vine, the mostos of which have long been highly esteemed in the locality. From here we drove to the neighbouring vineyards of Leon and Las Canas, in the Upper Balbaina district. The sun at this moment being at its fiercest, such "caballeros" as we encountered astride mule and donkey sought to shield themselves from its scorching rays by throwing their white linen jackets over their broad sombreros, while all mule or bullock drivers who were not sound asleep on their carts invariably halted at the ventorillos, or wayside drinking-places run up especially for the vintage, to drink some more reviving beverage than water. The soil of the Leon vineyard resembles that of the Carrascal district, and its mostos are held in the same esteem. Its little casa is after the Moorish style—blank walls, with here and there a loophole to serve as window, a low flat roof, and a solid square tower rising at one end. At Las Canas we were received by a trio of howling dogs, who sprang at us in company the full length of their chains, and it was only when they had been removed to a distance that we succeeded in gaining access to the courtyard of the casa. The vintage here was already over, and with the exception of a few butts of vino dulce from the Pedro Jimenez grape, it was all dry white wine which had been made. Las Canas, like all the more valuable vineyards of the Jerez district, is planted principally with the palomino vine, and produces a vino fino of great delicacy and character. We had already tasted various choice samples of it, free, of course, from added spirit, of different ages, including some of the amontillado type, in the bodega of the proprietor, Señor de Agreda, at Jerez. We gave the preference to a wine of twelve years old, of great delicacy and freshness of flavour, the older wines being in our judgment too pungent for ordinary drinking.

The casa de la vina of Las Cañas boasts a good-sized bodega of its own, where the mosto used formerly to ferment until racked from the lees the following spring. The proprietor, however, considers that the wine develops better if sent at once to Jerez to ferment in a larger bodega, and for several years past he has adopted this course. Like many of the casas hereabouts, that of Las Cañas has been designed as a summer residence for its owner. The ground floor, where the various processes of vinification are carried on, resembles a series of rude cloisters, with an occasional stone cross or niche for a statue of the Virgin above the arches, while the panels of the doors of the upper apartments are decorated with paintings of saints. The casa, moreover, has its abandoned little oratory. For years past only the workpeople have lived there, and now the vintage was over merely a single guard remained in charge.

There being neither mosto in the cellar, valuables in the house, nor well-to-do residents to protect, we were curious to know why three savage dogs were kept for the defence of the place. The reason given by the guard was this:—A few months ago a couple of red-sashed, black-bearded ruffians favoured him with a call, ostensibly to beg a draught of water. But, suddenly unsheathing their long knives, they threatened him with death if he did not surrender his watch and all the money he possessed. They had made a descent from the Sierra, and the guard being too insignificant a personage to carry off, they were willing to accept what he possessed, which amounted to 900 reals, or about nine guineas. The guard had no alternative but to comply, for, as the familiar proverb says, " Entre la espada y la pared"—meaning when between the sword and the wall refusal is out of the question. Having secured their booty, the robbers took their departure, vowing vengeance if the smallest alarm were given—a threat which the guard contemptuously disregarded, and luckily they were captured.

We now drove along solitary byroads through the entire of the Balbaina district, between steep banks planted as often with canes and aloes as with the prickly pear. A succession of large and handsome houses, generally with towers and encompassed by trees or surrounded by pleasant gardens, together with numerous smaller casas, were seen among the rolling sea of vines. They were almost invariably unoccupied; for the well-to-do-vineyard proprietors around Jerez dare not indulge in the pleasant patriarchal habit of sitting under their own vines and fig-trees. At length we reached the Tula vineyard in the lower Balbaina district, its casa resembling a Moorish castle with tall battlemented keep, surmounted by a turret, and flanked by small round towers with cupolas, and having even sham cannon peeping from its embrasures above clusters of brilliant rose laurels. The large almijar, too, was inclosed with pointed battlements. This costly whim appears to have brought ruin upon the late proprietor, and the vineyard passed into the hands of Señor Gonzalez. From the summit of the tower a view is gained in one direction over miles of undulating vineyards, while in another we catch sight of Cadiz and its bay, with Rota, famed for its Tent wine, Port St. Mary, and San Lucar, the long line of peaks of the Sierra de Jerez rising up in unbroken succession in an easterly direction. The Tula vineyard comprises about sixty acres, and at the time of our visit the vintage was drawing to a close, for the final carretadas of grapes were being trodden in the lagares. The capataz here was a great connoisseur in fighting-cocks, and had a collection of these pugnacious birds shut up in separate cages. With the lower-class Spaniards cock-fighting is almost as favourite a pastime as the national corrida de toros itself.

Our next excursion was to some of the vineyards of the plain to the east and north-east of Jerez. The vineyards situated on this side in the immediate neighbourhood of the town are believed to be the most ancient of all. At any rate, distinct allusion is made to them in a contemporary Arab account of the siege of Jerez in 1285 by the army of Jusuf, who is described as having the vines cut down preparatory to pitching his camp. The road we took was skirted on the left by a gigantic hedge of prickly pears, little short of twelve feet in height and solid in proportion, and which an enterprising elephant would find it difficult to break through. At the first vineyard, named "la vina enfrente de la venta de la Cuchara"—in other words, "the vineyard facing the Spoon wineshop"— where the vintage was at its height, we found the crop was estimated to be much larger in proportion than at any of the vineyards on the hills and slopes. This little plot of two-and-twenty acres, planted chiefly with the mantuo-castellano vine, produces in good years as many as 100 butts, or upwards of four and a-half butts per acre, of good white wine. Here, as elsewhere, we found very little yeso or gypsum being used, owing to the extreme dryness of the season.

Another small vineyard which we visited belonged to Senor Campo. It was planted with mantuos intermingled with palomino and other varieties, and showed evidence of very careful cultivation. The soil, of red earth, had the merit of retaining the moisture long after it had filtered through the chalky soil of the hills. An old-fashioned lever press was in operation here, which, although of no great power, required a couple of men to work a windlass, while three others set the lever in motion—a waste of labour which has its counterpart in the system of ploughing prevalent throughout Andalusia. The plough, which is of the rudest construction, is worked with a couple of oxen, and at least three, and frequently half a-dozen, or even more, of these primitive implements will follow one another in the same furrow to insure the soil being sufficiently turned, and yet even then the furrows are only a few inches deep.

After visiting other vineyards of the plain which promised scarcely the same satisfactory crops as those we had already inspected, we drove in the direction of the Cartuja, a finn old Carthusian monastery, which, in its day, was by far the wealthiest, as it was unquestionably the grandest, in this part of the country. Towards the latter part of our route the vineyard slopes of Mont Alegre, terminating in an abrupt point known as the Cabeza de la Azefia, together with those of Buena Vista, shut in the view on either hand. The vineyards formerly belonging to the monastery are some distance off in a northerly direction, and retain at the present day somewhat of their ancient reputation as well as their old name of " las vinas de la Cartuja." The ancient bodega, in which the monks could conveniently store a thousand butts of wine, is nearly perfect, otherwise the vast and highly ornate building, a monument of the piety or the fa-

naticism of past centuries, is now little else than a ruin. At its feet winds the Guadalete, the Arab's river of delight, and in the plain beyond one of the decisive battles of the world was fought, resulting in the defeat of Roderick, last of the Gothic kings, whose disasters have formed the theme of endless song and story.

V.—The Wines Of Jeeez—Blending Sheeey Foe Shipment.

System of Vitrification at Jerez—Vinos Finos and their Development into Falmas—Cause of Amontillado—Genuine Brown Sherries—Palos Cortados and Olorosos—Varieties of Rayasj Entre-finos, Bastos, Bedondos, and Abocados—Maladies of the Jerez Wines—The Bearing of them by Seasons and by Soleras—Vinos Dulces; Pedro Jimenez—Vino de Color—Classes of Jerez Wines Shipped to England— namely, Natural Wines, Vintage Wines, Solera Wines, and Blended Wines— Blending of Sherry in the Cosens Bodegas—The Process in all its Details—The Grand Finos, Amontillados, Olorosos, and Pasados of Cosens and Co.—Establishments of the Finn at Jerez and Puerto de Santa Maria.

Two distinct kinds of wine are made at Jerez—namely, the dry and the sweet—and to a limited extent a third variety known as vino de color. With respect to the dry wine as I saw it made in scores of vineyards, the grapes, when of a good variety and from a good vineyard, had previously been carefully looked over, all decayed bunches or berries being thrown aside. They had also been exposed to the sun for a moderate time before being trodden and pressed. Beyond this there was no difference whatever in the vinification— whether this was carried on in the vineyard or the bodega—of the very finest and the commonest wines, when produced from a first pressure of the fruit. Every one crushes the grapes in the same primitive way, uses much the same old-fashioned kind of press, and ferments his mosto under the same unscientific conditions. In the majority of

instances gypsum is sprinkled over the grapes either before or after they are partially trodden, the vineyards where this substance is not employed being comparatively few. There is not the smallest disguise about a practice dating back to very remote times, and by-and-by I shall show that the adherence to it by the winegrowers of the present day is unproductive of the slightest harmful result.

The mosto, after its transference to casks, which are never filled to within ten or fifteen gallons of their full capacity, is almost invariably removed from the vineyards to Jerez to ferment in the cool and capacious bodegas abounding there. This is all very well. Still, if some little attention were paid towards avoiding the previous exposure of the butts of mosto, often for one or two days together, to a temperature approaching fever heat at the casas of the vineyards— where Nature does much, man something, and science nothing at all—as well as during their transport to the bodegas, the fermentation would be conducted under more satisfactory conditions than can possibly be the case at present. In these bodegas the niosto remains completely isolated —it being disadvantageous to older wines to have new mosto fermenting beside them— with the bungs out of the butts, until the ensuing February or March. When the fermented wine is drawn from its lees into new casks—still with a vacant space left in them—a moderate quantity of aguardiente or grape-spirit is added to it. This varies with fine wines from under 1 up to 2 per cent., according to the nature of the vintage, and rises up to 3 or 4 per cent. for the commoner wines. The wine, with the bungs of the butts laid lightly over their holes, now enters a transition period, during which butts of wine from the same vineyard, and which have experienced precisely the same treatment, will develop totally different characteristics, while from 10 to 20 per cent. will become bad beyond recovery.

The vinos finos, or fine wines, grown on albariza soils, and made from the best varieties of grape, develop to a limited extent into amontillados, and eventually into olorosos, at times attaining this latter stage without passing through the former one. Such as have not undergone this development and remain vinos finos may be described as pale in colour, dry, soft, and delicate in flavour, spirituous yet entirely free from heat, and fresh to the taste. The finos passing into amontillados (so called from their resembling the fine old wines of Montilla) are classed as palmas, and the casks containing them have a sign resembling a single or double palm-leaf rudely chalked upon their front, according as they are regarded as single or double

D palma. Wine of this description is stouter, dryer, and more pungent in flavour than an ordinary fino, is of a more decided yellow or pale amber tinge, and when of the double palma type tastes riper, fuller, and altogether richer. The amontillado character results from the wines developing the mycoderma vina, or so-called flowers of wine, in the earlier stages of their existence. Under these conditions their alcohol, absorbing the oxygen of the atmosphere, becomes largely transformed into aldehyde, whence is due that marked etherous flavour commonly found in wines of this description.

The olorosos are known in their earlier stages as palos cortados, from the butts containing them being marked with an upright line intersected obliquely by a shorter one, and intended to indicate a cut stick. They are deeper in colour than the amontillados, have a nutty flavour, and are fuller, richer, and mellower to the taste, besides possessing an especially fragrant bouquet. Inferior wines are known as entre-finos, or middling fine; bastos, rough or coarse; redondos, round; and abocados, mild. In the bodegas, however, the above are simply grouped as single, double, and triple rayas, indicated respectively by one» two, or three perpendicular lines chalked upon the butts. Single raya is good-flavoured, dry, clean wine, but boasting no very prominent qualities, while double and triple raya are less clean and in other respects altogether inferior, decreasing, in fact, in quality

with the increase in the number of marks.

Although the Jerez wines frequently show early signs which indicate their future character, they cannot be classified with certainty until after their third year. At this age they may perhaps be considered fit for drinking, inasmuch as they will have completed their fermentation; still they will greatly improve with increasing years. Wine newly drawn off the lees, if of good quality, commands from £11 to £13 10s. the butt at Jerez, whereas inferior wines from the sandy soils can be bought at from £3 15s. to £6 the butt—these prices being exclusive of the cask. The D9w wine has to be carefully reared, subject to the accidents of falling off in quality, becoming scuddy, or turning sour, and with the certainty of wasting 3 per cent. per annum by the evaporation of its watery particles. The chances of the wine turning to vinegar from want of vinous strength may be met by the timely addition of spirit. It is scud, however, which is at once the arch-enemy and the constant dread of the almacenista, or winerearer, this malady attacking fine young wines, although less frequently, as well as the inferior ones. It often shows itself immediately after the wine has been racked, but more commonly during the hot weather. Generally it runs its course, no cure being known for it beyond the attempt to fine the wine with the whites of eggs.

A shipper buying a parcel of 100 butts of fine wine, the produce of a single vineyard, shortly after it has been racked from the lees, would regard the result as fortunate if two-thirds turned out well. These would, perhaps, comprise about a dozen butts of the oloroso type, a couple of dozen or more of the amontillado type, and about three dozen single raya, while the remaining third would belong partly to the inferior and partly to the worthless class. If, however, the wine were light in character it would probably produce no palo cortado or oloroso, in which case one-half of it might turn out amontillado and fine

The preservation and ageing of the Jerez wines are carried on after two dif-

ferent methods—that is to say, by seasons and by the system of soleras. The first consists in preserving each vintage intact, in which case the wine goes on acquiring much more consistency, colour, and aroma, while developing more subtle characteristics of the nature of balsams and essences. Generally individual growths aro not kept separate for more than from four to six years, when they commence to form part of the system of soleras, which has for its object the keeping up of certain distinct types of wine by rearing younger wines on the foundation of old ones, as already explained. When wine for shipment is drawn off in limited quantities and in equal proportions from the butts composing a solera, whatever is drawn from the cask containing the oldest wine, known as the solera madre (whose origin in rare instances will date as far back as a century and upwards), is replaced with the same kind of wine, but a year younger; and the same process goes on down to the bottom of the scale—a course which insures the respective ages of the wine being as far as possible preserved. This system is the one great speciality of the sherry district, and constitutes the principal wealth of the Jerez bodegas. It is not, however, invariably carried out in all its integrity, but is subjected to various modifications, wines drawn off being frequently replaced, not by wine of precisely the same character and almost the same age, but simply by analogous growths. It should be mentioned that the deposit which collects at the bottom of the casks is never by any chance removed, no matter how old the original wine may be. One marked advantage of the solera system to the sherry shipper is that it enables him to maintain the even character and quality of the wines which he supplies, irrespective of good and bad vintages.

Of Jerez sweet wines, or vinos dulces, the principal is Pedro Jimenez, made from the sweet translucent grape of the same name, which is exposed to the sun not unfrequently for a fortnight, before being trodden and pressed. To each butt of this wine about six or seven gallons of spirit are added, while other white wines made from different varieties of grapes have as much as twenty gallons mixed with each butt of must, to check the fermentation and thereby retain the requisite amount of saccharine. One-third of this quantity of spirit is poured into the cask as soon as a small portion of the must has been filled in, another third when the cask is almost half full, and the remainder when it is nearly three-quarters full.

Vino dulce is used to give softness and roundness to old and pungent wines, as well as to the cruder youthful growths, and it is remarkable how very small a quantity suffices perceptibly to modify these opposite characteristics. Amontillados that are highly esteemed at Jerez are invariably found too dry for English tastes, much as the connoisseurs of to-day may affect excessively dry wines. English correspondents often write for the driest varieties, still they rarely, if ever, get them. "Whenever I receive an order for the driest amontillado I have," remarked the principal shipper of this wine," I always put a gallon or more of dulce into it before shipping it, because I know that if I sent the wine in its natural state I should be certain to have it returned upon my hands." As little as one per cent. of dulce will impart a softness to the drier wines, which otherwise they only acquire after being, perhaps, half-a-dozen years in bottle. So decided is its influence on the finer wines that every shipping house of standing bestows especial care, if not upon the making of its own vino dulce, at any rate in the selection of the dulce which it uses. The larger firms, however, invariably prepare their sweet wine themselves.

Vino de color is composed of about nine parts of white wine mosto and one part of what is termed arrope, the latter produced by boiling in a large copper, and for a period of sixteen or eighteen hours, five butts of unfermented must, which thereby become reduced to one-fifth of the original quantity. Great care is taken to skim the liquid during this operation, so as to remove from it whatever impurities may be thrown off. The result is a deep brown bitterish fluid of the consistency of treacle, which, on being added to the mosto, ferments with it in the regular way. Vino de color, as its name implies, is used for imparting colour to young and undeveloped wines, the natural tint of which is pale and sickly-looking. When of high quality, however, it not only gives a pleasant tint to the wine, but imparts a certain amount of character to it as well.

Four different classes of dry Jerez wines are shipped to England—natural wines, understood to contain no added spirit; vintage wines, the produce of individual vineyards and occasionally of specific years; solera wines, such as fino, amontillado, and oloroso; and, finally, blended wines. The natural wines of which I speak are not the wines commonly advertised in England at low rates under that designation. Jerez wines perfectly free from spirit cannot possibly be sold cheap in England, because they require to be at least five years old; whereas the wines offered as natural are generally young, unripe wines, whose fermentation has not terminated, and which come far more frequently from Seville or La Mancha than from the Jerez district. Such wines are necessarily unwholesome, for heat revives their fermentative action, which completes itself in that delicate organisation, the human stomach.

The genuine natural wines of Jerez are carefully-selected varieties, arrived not only at an age when their fermentation is complete, but whose growth has, so to say, stopped—wines which, although remarkably delicate in flavour, still possess sufficient robustness to incur the risks of a sea-voyage without having alcohol added to them. The vintage wines, scarcely known at all in England, are the produce of good vineyards in the best viticultural districts, and have been reared intact, passing through a solera in the majority of instances, but subjected to no admixture with other wine, and receiving merely one per cent. of spirit at the time of being drawn from the lees. In the regular solera wines the distinct types into which the Jerez growths are divided are kept perfectly distinct, although the solera 'as it becomes diminished is replenished by the growths of varied years and districts, providing these are sufficiently approximate in character to the parent wine. In drawing these wines off for shipment, even as special types, they commonly receive a slight blend of dulce, being regarded, and in many instances with justice, as altogether too dry for English tastes, their pungency often rendering them somewhat unpalatable. The blended wines proper form the great bulk of the sherry shipped to England, and when of high quality and artistically treated are of splendid character, although perhaps less costly than exceptional examples of pure soleras.

Being anxious to witness in all its details this process of blending wine for shipment, I profited by an invitation from the resident partner of the firm of Cosens and Co., well known for the perfection of their blends, and whose business places them at only one remove from the head of tho list of sherry shippers. Most of the larger Jerez bodegas have their patches of flowers, their rows of orange-trees, their clusters or avenues of acacias, imparting a pleasant air to these huge wine-stores and their immediate surroundings. The Cosens bodegas, which have considerable architectural pretensions, are actually installed, as it were, in a large garden, whose palms and pines, pimiento, oleander, olive, and orange-trees, obscure anything like a complete view of these structures. They occupy three sides of this garden, the principal ones, a trio of lofty buildings parallel to each other —their high-pitched roofs supported by graceful stone columns with elegantly-carved capitals—being on our right hand after we have passed through the entrance gateway. Immediately in front of them is a wide colonnade stacked with casks seasoning with water. The nearest bodega is the one where the younger wines are stored. Here we see casks of wine being raised to the upper tiers by means of a movable iron crane—the only one to be found in the Jerez bodegas—instead of by the laborious, hazardous, and even dangerous method of a slanting tramway and ropes, in common use. Near by is the shipping bodega, where we find the butts in which the wine is about to be blended arranged all ready in rows. Our attention is first called to the elate containing instructions for the head cellarman, and from which we see that the blend includes four varieties, and these of the very best. Here, too, figures the brand which will be burned into the head of each cask, the shipping mark which will be cut into it near the bung, the number of butts, and, finally, the class and quantities of the respective wines of which the blend is to be composed. These include—

Amontillado pasado, 1820 7 arrobas.

Double palma (amontillado type), 1869.... 10 ,,

Single palma (fino) 12J ,,

Pedro Jimenez (vino dulce of the highest class).. i ,,

The wines being drawn from what are termed soleras on finings will have had their spirit added to them at the time they were fined. Owing to their age and superior quality, this, we were assured, would be equivalent to no more than a quarter, or at the utmost one-third, of an arroba to the butt of thirty arrobas. The alcoholic strength of a blended wine of this class will indicate about 32 degrees of proof spirit. The arumbadores, or cellarmen, who stand by in readiness, are all well-made, active men in the habitual uniform of the Jerez bodegas—caps, coloured shirts, light trousers, and the all-essential crimson or scarlet. sash; and certainly looking as though unlimited sherry agreed remarkably well with them. Tub-shaped funnels, inside which are fine hair sieves, serving in turn for all the butts, are fixed into the bungholes of the first and the third butts, and then the arumbadores commence drawing off the seven arrobas of ainontillado pasado in the following fashion:—A small tub is placed under the cask containing this wine to catch any that may chance to be spilt. One of the men then takes a clavo, or huge round nail bent at the end, which is spear-shaped, and a canuto, or short wooden tube in which

a cork has been inserted. Placing a jar that he holds in his left hand under the bung at the head of the butt, he draws the bung out with the clavo, catching in the jar whatever wine pours forth before he succeeds in ramming the canuto into the hole. The cork of the canuto is now removed, and, the jar being filled with the wine which gushes out, a second jar is slipped into its place at precisely the right moment, scarcely so much as a thimbleful of wine being wasted. The man's companions keep handing him fresh jars, and receiving from him those already filled. These they empty into the shipping butts. These so-called jars (jarras) are a kind of wooden pitcher bound round with iron, and having a sharp rim and iron handle. They hold threefourths of an arroba. The seven arrobas of pasado and the ten of double palma being filled in, only 11 out of the 12£ arrobas of single palma are added, so as to allow of an alteration in the character of the wine in case the blend should not turn out precisely as intended. The half-arroba of old Pedro Jimenez is being drawn from a cask on the upper tier by means of a metal syphon introduced into the bung-hole; after which the contents of one of the casks of blended wine are stirred well together with a wooden implement resembling a small oar. The amalgamation completed, some of the wine is drawn off and taken to the sample room, where it is inspected, tasted, and compared with the sample of a previous shipment; and then instructions are given either for some alteration in the blend or for adding the deficient arroba and a half of palma. The wine being perfectly bright and ready for shipment, the butts are filled up completely to the bungholes, and the wooden bungs driven tightly in so as to force any leakage arising from wormholes in the casks to show itself. The butts have now to be marked and branded, after which they will be sent off by the circular railway connecting the principal bodegas of Jerez with the Trocadero mole, near Cadiz.

The blending completed, we proceeded to the principal bodega to taste some of the more remarkable soleras of the

firm, thirteen of which, finos of singular delicacy and fragrance, and comprising an aggregate of 1,000 butts, were submitted to our inspection. We were also shown some fine amontillados of great age and ripeness, and remarkable softness of flavour; olorosos of ample roundness and aroma; with quite a collection of pasadoe, belonging to the first half of the present century, and including the years 1820, 1826, 1832, and 1837, together with Pedro Jimenez of almost fabulous antiquity—wines with pedigrees dating backwards for upwards of a hundred years, and the ruby brightness of whose tint, and rich liqueur-like flavour and consistency, time had enhanced rather than impaired. One of these wines, which was already so highly prized at the time of the French invasion that its owner buried it underground, had become highly concentrated, and was given to us to taste in drops.

When drawing sherry from the butt in the bodega for the purpose of tasting it an instrument termed a venencia is used. This is occasionally made in a somewhat rude fashion altogether of cane, but more generally consists of a long narrow silver receptacle attached to the end of a whalebone stick nearly three feet in length, and having a kind of handle at the opposite end to prevent it from accidentally slipping through the bung-hole into the butt when being wielded by an inexperienced hand. The operation, although it seems exceedingly simple, u one in fact requiring considerable skill. The arumbador, having removed the bung from the butt, takes a wine-glass in his left hand and the venencia in his right, holding the latter with his forefinger and thumb some few inches from the handle. He then lowers the end to which the silver receptacle is attached gently into the butt until it comes in contact with the wine, when he thrusts it suddenly down, and as soon as it is filled raises it again through the open bung-hole. Next, by means of a rapid movement of the thumb and forefinger by which the venencia is grasped, and a peculiar downward turn of the wrist of the same hand, he succeeds in deftly depositing the wine in a long trickling stream into the glass which he holds in front of him. The operation being commonly performed with much facility seems remarkably easy to accomplish, still the novice soon discovers that the requisite sleight-of-hand is only to be acquired after considerable practice.

The establishment of Messrs. Cosens and Co., in addition to their three large bodegas containing some 4,500 butts of wine, or less than half the firm's entire stock, comprises several secondary cellars wherein different types of wines are stored, as well as various bodegas in other parts of Jerez and at Puerto de Santa Maria, whence, by way of supplement to their vast Jerez trade, the firm ship between 1,200 and 1,300 butts of sherry annually. Here, too, is their cooperage—and here, as well as at Jerez, is the steaming apparatus for seasoning casks, by means of which no fewer than 125 butts are steamed at one time. While exposed to its action the heads of the casks often bulge outwards, and require to be forced into position again by a special apparatus. This steaming, which goes on for as long as eighteen hoiirs, combined with a thorough seasoning of the casks with water, renders any further seasoning with wine unnecessary. Every vacant space in the neighbourhood of the Jerez bodegas of the firm, including the long narrow avenues which separate one bodega from another, is crowded with piles of these seasoned casks, the total number of which must be many thousands. One very noticeable feature is that the different stages of preparation through which all these casks have passed, accord ing to the class of wine they are destined to contain, are recorded in every instance on the casks themselves.

In the rear of the trio of Jerez bodegas is a large open court shaded by picturesque trees, and here the steaming of the casks and various auxiliary operations are carried on. Here, too, the butts are repaired; here also are the smith's forge, the furnaces for heating the branding-irons, and the movable steam-engine for pumping up water for sea-soning the casks from an adjacent well. In this very complete establishment there are as many as thirteen mains available in case of fire, a precaution which originated during the time of the last Revolution, when no one's property in Jerez was safe.

VI.—The Assumed Unwholesomeness Op Sheeey.

The Careful Rearing which the Jerez Wines Undergo—The Great Age they Attain—The Blending of Sherry an Artistic Operation—The Late Outcry Against the Wiue—Highly-coloured Statements put forward and the motives which prompted them—Refutation of the Attacks—Gypsum in
Burton Beer — Scientific Investigation of the Plastering of Wine in
France—It is declared to be Innocuous—Fresh Investigations on the part of the French Government with a like result—The Sulphuring of
Wines—Opinion of the Vienna Jury upon the point.

I Have described the treatment which the Jerez wines experience while progressing towards maturity. Of the amount of attention bestowed upon the finer varieties in the earlier stages of their growth few have any correct idea. A mother scarcely tends her offspring with greater watchfulness and care. Plenty of air, a certain amount of light, and an equable temperature are all considered essential to their proper development, which goes on slowly, and by no means with invariable results. Often, before being considered fit to replenish a solera, the wines will pass through no fewer than four criaderas, which are really no many soleras at an earlier stage. During this period of probation their growth is most carefully watched. Arrived at four or five years of age, the wines may be drunk, but in justice to them they ought to be kept until they have attained their twelfth year; for not until then can they be had in high perfection—that is to say, delicate, with ample vinosity; full, with an unctuous limpidity; soft, yet richly aromatic, and at the same time perfectly free from that high pungent flavour which they acquire with length of years. The very finest growths will have had their 1 per cent. of spirit added to them when first drawn off the lees, and should they turn out grand wines they will rarely receive more; still, by the gradual evaporation of their watery particles, they will eventually develop as much as 34 per cent. of proof spirit, which will scarcely vary over a course of years. How long a robust Jerez wine will live, preserving within it the various elements of vinous vitality, it is scarcely possible to estimate. Wines the record of whose origin has been lost with the generations they have outlived are to be found in certain Jerez bodegas, sound and hale and seemingly with many long years still before them. Wines of a like antiquity, with the same amount of real vinous life in them, are not to be met-with in any other viticultural district of the world. But they remain simply studies for fortunate connoisseurs, being not only beyond the reach of the multitude, but even of the longest purses. Consolation, however, is to be had in the fact that, by reason of the powerful pungent flavour which these centenarian-wines develop, the more juvenile growths are far better adapted for ordinary consumption. Unquestionably, when met with at its best, under conditions in which few people drink it in England, because they lack the courage and common sense to pay the due price for choice qualities, sherry has but few superiors among the white wines of the world.

Sherry as exported is generally a blended wine, composed— unlike soleras of wines of one character, although of different ages—in the majority of instances, of several distinct types of wine. Recent vintages have character imparted to them by an admixture of some fine old variety, which again will have its pungency subdued by a moderate addition of dulce, while a touch of vino de color, if fine and old, will not only impart the required tint but improve the flavour. Aguardiente, or colourless spirit distilled from the grape, is added in a less or greater degree according to the character of the wine, which now undergoes the process of fining with the white of eggs and fuller's earth. When perfectly clean and bright it is drawn off into fresh casks, which if used for the first time will have undergone a thorough steaming on leaving the cooperage. Afterwards they will remain filled with hard water for the space of three months, then be again steamed, and subsequently be filled up with common wine for another three months, when they are considered thoroughly seasoned. The blending of sherry is a most delicate operation. It is not sufficient to be a good judge of wine and the possessor of an excellent stock to become a successful shipper; it is requisite to have the taste and judgment te blend your wines artistically. A writer on the subject has aptly remarked that you may give a score of men the requisite materials, but only one of them will be able to produce a picture; and so it is with reference to the more delicately blended types of sherry. The endless varieties of this wine to be found in a well-stocked bodega may be compared to so many musical notes which, in proportion to the skill with which they are arranged, conduce to a harmonious and successful result.

Every one will remember the late outcry raised against sherry, chiefly on the part of testimonial-purveying M.Ds. always ready to court publicity by rushing into print under the pretence of enlightening an unintelligent public. It was paraded in the papers, as though it were a new discovery, that gypsum was used when making the wine, and the inference was drawn that sherry is necessarily prejudicial to health. Among other highlycoloured statements was one, made with an air of authority, to the effect that the grapes for each butt of sherry invariably had from 30 to 40 lbs. of gypsum thrown over them prior to their being trodden and pressed, the main effect of which was to transform the tartar of the must into sulphate of potash, an aperient salt 3 to 14 lbs. of which were stated to be contained in every butt of this popular wine.

In common candour the author of this incredible misrepresentation ought not to have withheld from the public his qualifications to speak so confidently on the subject. He should have told them that he had visited Jerez under the auspices of certain shipping houses to whom he offered, if not to repeat the miracle of Cana, at any rate to produce amontillado by purely chemical agency—that he was provided with considerable funds for the purchase of scientific instruments which he was incompetent to use, and that he resided at Jerez in style for a period of three months at the expense of his principal patron, during which time he lost him half his vineyard's produce through the so-called amontillado which he professed to fabricate turning out such vile stuff that it could only be employed for rinsing casks with, while a further experiment which he made in the bodega of a second shipper resulted in transforming the wine into vinegar.

The public, knowing nothing of the motive which prompted these attacks upon sherry, naturally grew alarmed, and for a time the subject formed a common topic of conversation at all dinner-tables, where by the lady at your side you found sherry generally declined with thanks. Middle-aged gentlemen, too, perfectly hale and hearty on their daily pint of sherry, fancied. that perhaps for them a day of reckoning might be near. The alarm, however, soon subsided, and people returned to their old love; yet it is none the less desirable that the truth of the matter should be made known, and the public mind disabused of any latent fears upon the subject.

During my sojourn at Jerez I paid particular attention to this plastering question, saw the gypsum applied in almost a hundred instances, and questioned the capatazes in scores of vineyards. I may state as within my own knowledge that gypsum is by no means invariably used in the vinification of sherry, some thousands of butts having been made during the past and former years at Jerez without a particle of this substance. I have, moreover, ascertained by personal observation that when it is employed only a small quantity—a few pounds per butt of 108 gallons—is used. Undoubtedly gypsum is applied in the great majority of instances; still I can confidently assert that 6 lbs. per butt may be regarded as the extreme quantity used in dry seasons, and that double this quantity, or perhaps rather more, would be the average amount employed in years when great dampness prevails. For the sake of argument, however, I will assume the extreme quantity ever asserted as being employed to have been used, and will show, not by pseudo-scientific statements, but on evidence recorded in text-books and accepted by *savants* of the highest standing, that its employment is perfectly harmless.

The detractors of sherry can scarcely be aware that the superiority of Burton bitter beer is owing to the large amount of gypsum contained in the-water of the Trent, and that quite as much of this innocuous substance enters into a pint and a-half of that excellent beverage as into any bottle of sherry in existence. In one respect gypsum acts, with regard to the fermentation of beer, precisely in the same way as it acts with reference to that of wine—that is to say, it checks over-activity by counteracting the influence of the excess of nitrogenous matter present alike in wort and must, and which troubles bitterbeer brewers in the form of gluten and the Jerez wine-growers in the shape of albumen. So important an element, indeed, is gypsum in the brewing of beer that many Scotch and other brewers add it in considerable quantities to the water which they employ.

Not merely is gypsum largely used by brewers, but all the wine-growers of the South of France have recourse to it. Some years ago proceedings were taken against the latter, under the pretence that the use of gypsum constituted an adulteration, and the matter eventually came on appeal before the tribunal of Montpellier, which appointed three distinguished French chemists, MM. Chancel, Berard, and Cauvy, who had mado wine their especial study, to investigate and report upon the subject. Singularly enough, these gentlemen made their experiments upon wine containing as nearly as possible the same proportion of gypsum as according to the most extravagant estimate enters into a butt of sherry—namely, 401bs. to the 108 gallons. The wines they analysed had been plastered to the extent of 40 grammes per litre, which is at the rate of almost 20,000 grammes, or 401bs., to the 484 litres comprised in the 108 gallons which a butt of sherry contains.

The analyses of these wines showed that the sample to which ordinary plaster had been applied contained 1-240 grammes of sulphate of potash per litre, and that another sample of wine made with prepared plaster contained T828 grammes of sulphate of potash per litre, which gave in the first instance less than 600 grammes, or under ljlb., and in the second less than 900 grammes, or under 21bs., in the 108 gallons, which is very different from the 141bs. result put forward by individuals who, even if competent, could never have taken the trouble to perform an analysis for themselves.

The French chemists reported—first, that plastered wine contains no new mineral substance, implying that none of the plaster remained in the wine in solution; secondly, that the amount of plaster—40 grammes to the litre, equivalent to 401bs. per butt—could have no harmful result as it became completely transformed, and that the only objection that could be urged against sulphate of potash was that it is slightly aperient, as are also the tartrates themselves upon which the gypsum acts. Brillat-Savarin had a fantastical objection to grapes, and used to say that he did not care to take his wine in pills. Here the process is reversed, and the pills are taken in the wine.

Guided by the scientific evidence, the tribunal of Montpellier decided that the employment of gypsum during vinification could not be regarded as an adulteration, and, further, that it was not injurious to health.

Not entirely satisfied with the result, the French Government took the matter up, ostensibly in the interest of the army and navy, and appointed a scientific commission still further to investigate the subject. This commission eventually decided that plastered wines containing sulphate of potash in no larger quantity than at the rate of 4 grammes per litre, which is more than double the quantity found in the samples analysed by the French chemists, might be safely admitted to consumption in the army and navy, and to-day fully two-thirds of all the wine made in France is made by the aid of plaster.

The assumed sulphuring that sherry undergoes is limited, so far as the better-class wine is concerned, to the preliminary purification of the casks for containing the mosto by burning a sulphur match inside them, according to a practice prevalent all over the world. Occasionally common Jerez wines are sulphured, just as all the sweeter Sauternes are—in the latter case to check the fermentation and prevent all the sugar turning into alcohol. This question of sulphuring wines was fully discussed by the l scientific members of the wine jury at the Vienna Exhibition with reference to some magnificent " Auslesen" from the vineyards of the Rheingau exhibited by Herr Wilhelmj (priced from 15s. to 45s. per bottle), which had had their fermentation cheeked by sulphur. The jury agreed with the opinion expressed by chemists of repute that no harm can result from the practice provided the sulphuric acid is afterwards got rid of, as it easily can be, byproper tapping. It would appear, therefore, from the investigations of competent scientific authorities, that the outcry raised against sherry was an utterly baseless one.

VH.—The Bodegas In The Old Moorish Quarter Of Jerez.

A Great Jerez Shipping Establishment—The Offices, Press-house, and Cooperage—The Stables, the Shipping Bodega, and the Sample-rooms—Maturing of the Commoner Wines—The Bodega de la Union and its Annexes—Huge Tuns known as Los Apostoles —The Parte Arroyo and Sefior Gonzalez' Blind Bargain — The Constancia Bodega and the Romano Wine—The Bodega de los Ciegos and the A. B. Wine—The Bodega Vieja and Sefior Gonzalez' " Piano"—The Bodega de la Rosa and the Methusalem, Noah, and La Rcyua Wines—The Bodega Reservada, with its Napoleon III., Muscatel, and Fragrant Tio Pepe Wine9—The Blending Cellar, Casksteaming Apparatus, and Distillery—Railway Incline—Other Bodegas of the Firm at Puerto de Santa Maria, San Lucar, Seville, and Montilla— Sefior Domecq's Bodegas—Steaming and Gauging the Casks—The Cooperage—Fine Amontillado and Oloroso—The Famous Napoleon Wine, and its Christening by Marshal Soult—Other Remarkable Wines—Sefior Domecq's Criaderas—The Bodegas of Vergara, Robertson, and Co.—Visit paid to them by Ferdinand VII.—Superior Wines of the old Jerezano Type.

During the year 1873 thers-were exported from Jerez alone no fewer than 68,500 butts, or nearly 7 millions of gallons, of sherry. While about seven-eighths of this large quantity of wine went to the United Kingdom and the colonies, a like proportion came from the bodegas of about twenty Jerez firms. The establishment of one of the principal of these, that of Messrs. Cosens and Co., I have already described, and I now propose speaking of the remaining ones, indicating in a measure the specialities for which each is remarkable.

Forty years ago a new firm of sherry shippers established themselves at Jerez in a very modest way, for their first year's shipments comprised merely ten butts of wine. During 1873, however, their shipments had risen to 10,000 butts, and to-day the firm of Gonzalez, Byass, and Co. are the owners of the largest establishment in all Jerez, where colossal establishments are the rule.

Descending a flight of steps leading from the terraced Alameda vieja, one finds oneself in front of a pillared gateway giving access to the premises of the firm in question, which cover an area of sixteen acres, and comprise, in addition to an open press-house with numerous lagares, nearly a score of bodegas, a distillery, an admirably-organised cooperage, and various complementary workshops, together with steam-power and all the requisite mechanical appliances, including even a railway siding; so that here the processes of cast-making as well as wine-making, and the rearing, blending, and shipping of wines, may be followed from beginning to end, and a complete idea gained of what a great sherry shipper's establishment is like. Immediately inside the courtyard are the offices, under the arcade of which some half-dozen wine-brokers, with the necks of numerous sample bottles peeping from their side-pockets, are waiting an audience, while a group of rustic mayetos, who have sold their vintages to the firm, are taking their turn at the cashier's desk to be paid. Passing through the clerks' office, partitioned off into numerous little cabinets, we enter the sanctum of the firm, the walls of which are hung with portraits of past and present partners, and paintings, plans, and maps, more or less relating to the production of a wine which has raised an Andalusian village almost to the rank of a city. The senior partner is engaged in testing samples brought by a wine-broker, and, this little operation over, he courteously volunteers to conduct us through the vast establishment of which he is the head. We pass the porter's house, whereby is a charming flower-walk, skirted by palms and orange-trees, and bordered on the one side by a trellised arcade overgrown with vines. Hereabouts is a huge water-tank supplied from a deep well, the water of which is specially used for seasoning the casks. Passing the great square and circular bodegas, the garden and the fountain, the stables and the wheelwright's shop, the railway siding and the steep tramway incline, we make our way to the press-house, where mules keep arriving with baskets of grapes, which, after being weighed in a primitive fashion by the aid of a beam supported on a couple of men's shoulders, are thrown into one or other of the seven lagares and trodden and pressed. A few paces off is the store-place for American oak staves, of which the casks are made, and which remain stacked up here in huge piles until they have "lecome thoroughly seasoned, while beside them lie innumerable long bundles of osier, for making the wooden hoops. The staves come in shiploads

from New York, and Messrs. Gonzalez have a large depot for them at Puerto Real, fifteen miles distant from Jerez on the Cadiz line of railway. In a neighbouring shed a sawmill is at work cutting these staves to precise lengths; after which they are sent in truck-loads up a steep incline to the cooperage, the traction being accomplished by steam-power obtained from an adjacent engine, which is principally employed in pumping water into the reservoir already mentioned.

The cooperage occupies a vast open space surrounded on all sides by a broad colonnade, where scores of coopers are engaged trimming and planing the staves into shape with quaint-looking tools, which they use with singular skill and certitude. This work is principally accomplished by men sitting astride slanting benches, the lower ends of which grasp the staves, while the men trim and plane them, both their hands being disengaged for this purpose. After the sides, where the staves join together, have been carefully adjusted, and every little hole and crevice has been plugged with pieces of cane, a cooper proceeds to put the casks together, the staves being arranged so as to be perfectly close at the top and spread out at the bottom. Some iron hoops being temporarily wound round them to hold them firmly together, the staves are so placed as to encompass a blazing fire, under the influence of which they are bent; and the cask being thus formed, it is kept in shape by permanent iron hoops. The charred wood is now scraped from the inside of each butt, which next has its bottom and top inserted, the edges of its staves bevelled, and finally its bung-hole drilled. The cask is now ready for being steamed, and at Messrs. Gonzalez' this very essential process is accomplished by machinery, which causes the casks to revolve in an eccentric circle by the aid of steam-power. The butts subsequently remain filled with water for three months, and then with wine for a like period, after which they are branded, and are ready for use.

On our way to the bodegas we glance at the stables, but the score of mules and

half-a-dozen horses are all out at work. Two superannuated animals are the only occupants—a whit horse, whose large head and thick arched neck indicated the ancient Andalusian breed, and a dropsical old donkey who is contentedly munching his chopped straw. Ascending an adjacent flight of steps, we find ourselves in an annexe of the vast extraction bodega, where wines destined for shipment are kept. The annexe is used for the washing of old casks by rocking them backwards and forwards with a couple of long chains inside, after they have been filled with water. Leaving this department we enter the many-aisled shipping bodega, containing some 5,000 butts of wine of all descriptions, which are being got ready for shipment as required. On one side a gang of men are engaged in raising casks to the third or ipper tier, by means of an improvised tramway incline. In another aisle some half-dozen cellarmen are making up five-and-twenty butts of Royal Pale, while at the northwest side of the building others are emptying casks of ordinary wine into a receptacle communicating by pipes with the vats in the blending cellar below, whence butts of newlyblended wine keep arriving by means of a powerful steam-lift at the rate of a score in as many minutes. As we leave this bodega on our left hand is a gallery containing thirteen enormous tuns of vino dulce, four of them holding no less than thirty-two butts, or nearly 3,500 gallons each. To the right we have the shipping office, with the testing and the shipping samples rooms, the latter containing some thousands of bottles, on each of which is specified the mark, price, and destination of the wine shipped, the date of its leaving the bodega, and the name of the vessel it was despatched by.

After traversing a corner of the shipping cellar we enter another annexe of that gigantic bodega. This is a long building, with a galvanised iron roof attracting the heat, and thereby helping to mature the commoner class of wines stored beneath it, which ordinarily remain here for three or four months. Numerous apertures in the sides of the building allow a full current of air to sweep through it, causing an evaporation of 2 per cent. during the three months, or double what it would be in any ordinary bodega. In front of this annexe is a large circular structure with a sloping metal roof devoted to the same object and holding some five or six hundred butts of wine. The next building we visit is the Bodega de la Union, the contents of which continually vary, and where at present wines of various descriptions—dry, sweet, and "color"—with mosto of last year from the Romano and A. B. vineyards, are stored. To the left is the Salon annexe, containing about 300 butts of mosto vintaged quite recently, while to the right is another annexe, known as Los Apostoles, and so named from twelve huge casks containing pale, gold, and amber-coloured sherries, fino, amontillado, oloroso, Pedro Jimenez, and muscatel. These casks hold 1,420 gallons each, and are ranged in rows of six on either side of a gigantic tun of 3,500 gallons, carved over with bunches of grapes and vine-leaves, evidently of German origin, and recalling those famous examples of the cooper's art occasionally met with in the mediaeval cellars of the Fatherland. Although of fine character, none of the wine in these monster receptacles equals in interest that contained in some venerable butts, perfectly black with age, which, ranged in tiers in a corner of the same cellar, are known as the Parte Arroyo, after a widow of that name, from whom they were purchased many years ago. She was bent on retiring from business, and demanded.£10,000 in gold for the contents of her cellar, which, however, she resolutely refused to open for inspection until she had the money in hand. Senor Gonzalez boldly accepted this blind bargain, paid the price, and received the key of the bodega, which was found to contain one hundred butts of very fine old wine, worth far more than the price demanded. Only a comparatively small number of these butts now remain.

Crossing the road running in front of the Union Bodega we enter another of these light and lofty wine-stores with rows of portly butts ranged in seemingly endless succession, known as the Constancia, where the fine old wines from the Romano vineyard, purchased from the family of this name, are stored in soleras of four tiers. The Romano is a full-bodied wine, soft in flavour and invariably deep in colour, arising partly from the admixture of Pedro Jimenez grapes, and partly because none of the grapes of this vineyard are picked until late in the season, in order that they may be thoroughly matured. Even then they are exposed to the sun for a longer time than is customary-with grapes from other vineyards. A thousand butts of this wine, itsaverage strength indicating 36 deg. of proof spirit, are stored here unmixed with any other vintage. From the Constancia bodega we passed through a narrow triangular courtyard into the Bodega de los Ciegos, holding some 1,200 butts of very fine wine. One sample that we tasted was pale but remarkably brilliant in colour, and had something of the character of manzanilla about it. The wine from the A. B. vineyard, the soleras of which are kept here, was equally pale and bright. It had, moreover, a fine, fresh, delicate flavour, leaving behind it a slight and pleasant bitter-almond taste, in addition to which it exhaled a peculiarly rich aroma.

In the adjoining Bodega vieja, the original cellar of the firm (a comparatively small structure with a low blackened roof), we ran through the scales of what Senor Gonzalez terms his " piano," meaning by this twenty-one selected butts of wine produced in a vineyard owned by Senor Bomero Valdespino. For upwards of twenty years the firm have purchased the entire produce of this vineyard, the mosto of which is remarkably rich and sweet, and yields a wine of much distinction. In 1853 Senor Gonzalez commenced to set aside a butt of this wine after it was a certain number of years old, a practice continued every year up to the present time. Ho expresses himself confident that in every instance the wine has had less than 1 per cent. of spirit added to it; and yet when tested at five years old it showed 27 deg. of proof spirit, at ten years 28 deg., at fifteen years 30 deg., at twenty years 33 deg., and at twenty-five years 36 deg. This gradual increase of its alcoholic strength can only have arisen from the conversion of its saccharine into spirit, combined with the evaporation of its watery parts, and the consequent concentration of the wine. Tasting the samples, we found the youngest delicate, and of a certain freshness of flavour which gradually became more tonieal as the wines advanced in years until about half-way up the scale, when they began to reveal a bitter taste, although still retaining a peculiar softness. The gradations of colour and flavour were perfect, and very minute. With every year of increasing age the light tint of the wine slightly darkened. just as its flavour grew the merest trifle more pronounced.

Perhaps the most curious wines in Sefior Gonzalez' collection are some dating from 1809 down to comparatively recent years, stored in the Bodega de la Rosa. Here we tasted some remarkably fine wine from a solera originated in 1847, and then some very old wine known as Methusalem, of whose great age there is no record. It is exceedingly dark in colour and pungent and spirituous in flavour, as becomes a wine of such archaic origin. Its neighbour, Noah, not boasting the same length of years, could be partaken of with less hesitation, although a still rich powerful wine. We next tried some fine old-fashioned East India sherry which had received a small addition of dulce and vino de color, and had long since been its voyage to India and back. A captivating wine called La Reyna, of a bright deep topaz tint, had great body, and was deliciously round and mellow; while a wine of 1828 proved too dry to be palatable, and, like most of the older vintages, was only used, we were told, for blending. Passing from the Bodega de la Eosa into the Bodega Reservada—the last of the series—we were invited to taste the favourite wine of a former partner in the firm, and were surprised to find that, although of the juvenile age of two-and-thirty years, it had acquired a peculiarly disagreeable flavour too much like that of tar. Some remarkable wine, named after Napoleon III., and believed to be fully a century old, was next offered to us, and proved to be one of those venerable concentrated wines whose powerful flavour almost takes away the breath. It had passed through the amontillado and oloroso stages, and had now got into what is known as the old sherry type—that is to say, it was very deep in colour, full and pungent to the taste, and could boast of a powerful aroma. After these excessively dry wines wo essayed some muscatel from the Ducha vineyard. At five years old the wine was very soft and luscious; at eight years it was still very sweet, but more vinous and darker in colour; while at fifteen years much of its sweetness had gone, and its tint was almost black. Some muscatel from Romano sixty years of age had consumed the greater part of its saccharine, and become a perfect liqueur. After tasting the muscatel a glass of light Jerez wine, known as Tio Pepe, seven years old, and containing only 25 deg. of proof spirit, proved agreeably refreshing. This wine has the bouquet and much of the flavour, including all the delicacy, of the rarer growths of the Rhine, coupled with that peculiar soft almond taste which these latter wines not unfrequently develop. and shipjjers of sherry, have as many as 600 people at work. In addition to the bodegas of the head establishment, the abandoned convent of San Domingo at Jerez has been turned by them into a bodega for the storing of wines from their own vineyards, which, kept apart from other vintages, are shipped to England under their distinctive names. The firm further possess bodegas at Puerto de Santa Maria, San Lucar, Seville, and Montilla. Not only have they agencies all over Europe, but in South America, British North America, and the United States. Theirstock comprises 18,000 butts, or nearly two millions of gallons of wine, and their Jerez establishment is certainly one of the greatest in the world.

Leaving the half-dozen remaining bodegas unvisited, we now direct our steps to the blending cellar, beneath the prolonged colonnade, which, from its succession of columns and vast length—600 feet—is jocularly known as the Rue de Rivoli. At one end of it scores of casks are being steamed by machinery, while along it, and beneath the adjacent trees, thousands of butts, undergoing the necessary seasoning with water, are stacked in tiers. Other casks under the colonnade are seasoning with common wine, and at its farther end some hundred butts of prensa—wine from the final pressing of the grapes—are waiting their turn to be distilled into spirit. A powerful hydraulic press has been erected for squeezing the lees of the wine perfectly dry, also for the purpose of distillation. In the blending cellar, butts of common wine are being rapidly filled from the taps of half-a-dozen of the seventeen large blending vats containing their 120 butts; or more slowly, by means of jars, when a mixture of several varieties has to be made. In the adjoining distillery a large still and rectifying apparatus are in full operation, but the fire of the huge iron caldron in which arrope is boiled for vino de color is unkindled. All that now remains for us to visit is the steep railway incline, down which butts of wine are being whirled on trucks for conveyance by the train in waiting below, which will convey them to the Trocadero mole, whence they will be shipped to England and elsewhere.

Messrs. Gonzalez, who are at the same time growers, rearers, s

Situated nigh to the establishment of Gonzalez, Byass, and Co., in the old Moorish quarter of the sherry capital, and crowning a corresponding height to that from which the ancient Alcazar, in all the pride of fresh whitewash, glares down upon the town, are the capacious bodegas of Sefior Domecq. Passing through the usual green gateway and paved courtyard, the low arcade of which is closely stacked with caskstaves, a narrow passage conducts the visitor to the escritorio and the rooms, handsomely decorated with encaustic tiles, which are devoted to brokers' and shipping samples. The latter contain some thousands of uniform bottles, comprising samples of all the wine shipped by the house for several years back, duly dated and classified. Behind is a small floral parterre, succeeded by an avenue of acacia and orange trees, with bodegas ranged along either side, and having at the farther end a gateway crowned by a statue of Bacchus, cup and thyrsus in hand, astride the conventional wine-cask. Beyond this gateway and extending down the slope of the hill is a beautiful garden, the view from which over the neighbouring plain is bounded by a long sweep of vine-clad slopes and undulating country.

The first bodega we enter is the one where wines are prepared for shipment—a vast building of six aisles, between 500 and 600 feet long, 120 feet broad, and lofty in proportion, and in which upwards of 3,500 butts of wine are stored ready for exportation. Beyond rises the wide, light, and airy Bodega de la Luz, built on a steep slope, and having three tiers of vaults, used chiefly as spiritstores, at the farther end. Close at hand, and nigh to where the several processes of cleansing, steaming, and watering the casks are being carried on, some men are determining the capacity of the newly-made butts, which, as Sefior Domecq does not approve of the gauging system, is done by filling the casks with water. Should a butt be found to contain even a gallon more than its proper quantity, it is allowed to pass, but the smallest deficiency leads to the cask being altered by removing the hoops and replacing a particular stave by a slightly larger one. Bound three sides of the adjoining cooperage runs an arcade, under the shade of which scores of men are busy as bees trimming, planing, and plugging the staves, hammering the iron hoops into form and punching holes in them, and adroitly putting the portly butts together.

Sefior Domecq's finest wines are stored in a bodega facing his shipping cellar. Among the numerous samples we here tasted was some fine amontillado which had been on a solera for fiveand-twenty years, and had acquired an exceedingly dry and highly tonical flavour. A wine from the Macharnudo vineyard, fifty years of age, and of the robust oloroso type, was remarkable for body and roundness. Another wine, three-quarters of a century old, proved excessively pungent; but we were assured that, after being in bottle for about five years, it would become as soft as oil. The wine on which Sefior Domecq most prides himself is one belonging to a solera dating back to 1730— nearly a century and a-half ago—of which only eight of the original twenty-five casks remain. These butts are very rarely drawn from, still their contents gradually decrease through evaporation, and from time to time some very fine old wine has to bo added to them. The liquid proved to be a veritable essence, very deep in colour, of an oleaginous-like fulness, and a pungency of flavour that asserted itself the instant the wine touched the lips. The alcoholic strength of this venerable wine has been periodically tested, and for a considerable period has remained stationary at 43 degrees of proof spirit. During recent years only three quarter-casks of it have been sold—one to the late Duke of Hamilton, another to a retired wine-merchant named Nisbet, who paid. £1,000 for it, or at the rate of £6 5s. per bottle *in loco*—the highest price paid for a wine on record, being 25 per cent. more than was obtained a few years ago for the famous Chateau Lafite of the grand Comet vintage of 1811—and a third to the late Emperor of the French, whose reason for securing some of the wine was possibly because it was named after Napoleon I. When Marshal Soult was at Jerez in 1808 he seems to have visited the Domecq bodega, and after tasting the most ancient wine stored there, out of compliment to it wrote the word "Napoleon" on the head of the cask with a piece of chalk. The marshal's caligraphy was of the worst, still the inscription was preserved for many years as a souvenir of his visit, and the wine has ever since been known by the name he gave to it. When the great emperor's star paled, other casks of the same wine were christened Wellington, Nelson, Pitt, and Fox. Two other casks subsequently had the names of former partners in the houso of Domecq and Co. bestowed upon them, one being called Buskin, after the father of the author of *Modern Painters*. A butt of very fine old sweet wine preserved in the same bodega enjoys the honour of being called, after the Finest Gentleman in Europe—Georgius Quartus Rex. Senor Domecq prides himself on his criaderas, which are distributed over a couple of bodegas; the first a square lofty building of eight aisles, situated immediately beyond the solera bodega, and capable of holding 2,500 butts; while the second, which has room for a couple of thousand casks, is detached from the rest of the establishment. The nursing system is here in full operation, the wines stored passing through as many as four criaderas before going to a solera, and remaining invariably a year or more in each. Some of the wine in these nurseries had been vintaged as recently as 1872, but the larger portion was five and six years old. In order that the wine used to replenish a solera may be of equal quality, it is carefully blended beforehand, ten gallons being taken from one cask and ten from another, and so on through the entire criadera.

At the extremity of the old Moorish quarter of Jerez are the bodegas of Messrs. Vergara, Robertson, and Co., originally in the occupation of the late Sefior Domecq. Passing through a small courtyard, one enters the principal cellar, a lofty, wide, and well-proportioned structure—at one time the largest that existed in Jerez—with the unusual appurtenance of a gallery at the farther end, erected for the accommodation of Ferdinand VII., father of the ex-Queen Isabella, when he honoured this bodega with a visit and tasted its rare old vintages. Messrs. Vergara and Co. are famous for wines of the old Jerezano type—superior rayas of rich flavour, ample body, and perfect rotundity. In connection with the Vergara bodegas is an extensive cooperage, and arcades crowded to the roof with new casks passing through one or other of the usual seasoning processes.

VIII.—Some Othek Jerez Bodegas.

The Establishment of Sefior Misa, Condc de Bayona, its Array of Bodegas and Monumentnl Tower—Its more remarkable Soleras—Garvey and Co.'s Monster Bodega—Their Soleras of Choice Amontillados—The Old Brown Sherry of the Prince of Wales—Youthful and Matured Montilla Wines— The Ancient Jerez House of Hauric—Its Blended Wines, Amontillados, and Olorosos—Don Diego de Agreda's Choice Soleras—His Mauresque House and Handsome Garden—Sefior Julian Pemartin's Amontillados, Vinos de Pasto, and Jerezano Wines—The Venerable Soleras of Sefior Jose' Pcmartin— Mr. K. Davies's Bodega—His San Lucar and Madeira Vineyards—His Delicate Amontillados and Fragrant Finos and Manzanillas —Mr. J. C. Gordon's Olorosos, Potent Brown Sherry, and High-class Finos —Sefior J. J. Vegas's Choice and Robust Rayas—Wisdom and Warter's Montilla Finos—Their Empcrador and Sweet Pedro Jimenez— Mr. R. Ivison's Wines of the old Jerezano Type—His Mode of Developing the Seville Wines—Webber and Co.'s Finos—Mackenzie and Co.'s Manzanillas, Amontillados, and Centenarian Olorosos—Heywnrd and Wilson's Finos and Manzanillas, their Montilla and old Jerezano Wines—Matthiesen and Furlong's Bodegas in the Jesuit Church and Convent—Their Vineyard in the Cuartillos and its Fino Wine—Sefior Ysasi's Finos and Amontillados—Cramp and Suter's Fino Soleras and Rare Old Wines— The Jerez Almaccnistas and the Establishment of Sefior Sanchez Romate.

On arriving at Jerez by railway, among the first objects that attract one's attention is a lofty square tower, rising above an extensive range of carefully-ordered buildings, situate within a few hundred yards of the station. These are the premises of Senor M. Misa, Conde de Bayona, and one of the magnates of the sherry metropolis. In this striking assemblage of bodegas as many as 18,000 butts of wine arc stored, and connected with them are the usual cooperage, carpenters' and smiths' shops, departments for steaming and seasoning casks, and all the necessary adjuncts to a shipping establishment on a vast scale. On our visit we passed through the different offices, comprising the escritorio or counting-house, the private room of the principal of the firm, the apartment in which brokers who come to offei wines are received, and the sample-room in which the wines in question are tasted, together with the shipping sample room, containing Bome 11,000 samples of wine exported during the past five years. The labels on all the bottles indicate alike the number of the invoice, the quantity of casks shipped, with the date of shipment, and the name of the port to which and of the party to whom they were shipped. The advantage of this system is that when a wine-merchant desires to repeat an order reference has merely to be made to the invoice, which indicates the precise blend of the wine, and to the sample which has been retained, enabling any alteration that is found necessary to be readily made.

'We first inspect the lofty sis-aisled Bodega vieja, containing 3,000 butts of wine in soleras, comprising fines, amontillados, and olorosos. Two thousand of these are finos ranging from 5 to 40 years of age, and passing through four successive stages, while the amontillados and olorosos pass through three, thus enabling the older soleras to be replenished with comparative facility, and insuring a uniform quality of wine. The most noticeable among these soleras are what is termed the 150. fino and the 1/30 gogolio, both very superior wines. No aguardiente is added to these soleras, the average alcoholic strength of which ranges no higher than from 27 to 28 deg. of proof spirit. A different system is followed with the so-called Royal solera, a fino selected and established in 1853 from several thousand butts of dos palmas of the 1846 vintage. This solera, which is of the highest character, is only replenished by dos palmas of vintages fully ten years old. Its bouquet, softness, and delicacy are almost unrivalled, in addition to which its alcoholic strength indicates only 25 deg. of

proof spirit. An adjoining smaller bodega, holding 800 butts, contains some of the rarer soleras of the house, purchased five-and-forty years ago, and of acknowledged antiquity even at that epoch. In this bodega are installed the superb oloroso solera, the *non plus ulira* of 1815, the famous amontillado of 1820, and the superior palo cortado of 1831, with several other wines in the old Jerezano style of the vintages of 1824, 1843, and 1846. This and other cellars of the house contain 1,600 butts of oloroso soleras, ranging from 8 to 60 years old, and which are kept up by means of the three successive stages to which we have already alluded.

Traversing the principal courtyard, where we get a glimpse of a couple of dark-eyed Spanish damsels nimbly knitting beneath a shady green arbour, we inspect the little Lara Bodega, a recent purchase by the house, and containing 600 butts of young wines, and next visit the Badel Bodega, holding some 2,500 butts, where amontillados and superior rayas—that is, wines of the old Jerezano type—are stored. Some of these latter wines were purchased in 1846, when they were already old, and they certainly are remarkable for their richness and fragrance. In this cellar some old East India sherry of great age and peculiar aroma is preserved. From here we pass through the low, irregularly-built, and somewhat picturesque Fontan Bodega, devoted to sweet wines, including fine and rare Pedro Jimenez and moscatel—some of the soleras of the former not having been refreshed for many years—and then proceed to the grand Bodega nueva, the largest but one in all Jerez, and holding as many as 8,000 butts of wine, including every sweet and dry variety. Here are several soleras of Montilla from the pagos known as the Zapateros, which enjoys the reputation of producing the very finest wine; with other soleras of Montilla, exceedingly light and delicate in flavour, from the Cabra district, where Senor Misa annually secures the produce of a very large vineyard. This bodega also contains dry and sweet wines of the Arcos district, where Senor Misa possesses an estab-

lishment at which several hundred butts of wines are vintaged annually.

Under the spacious exterior arcade of the Bodega nueva, looking on to a long paved court bordered with orange-trees, and where oak staves imported direct from the United States are stacked, a vast number of casks undergoing the tedious but allnecessary seasoning process are piled. These casks, after remaining filled with water for from four to six months, are transferred to the large cellar opposite, containing several thousands of butts, hogsheads, and quarter-casks, where they are filled up to the bunghole with wine, in which condition they complete their seasoning. A double line of rails, which forms a junction when passing beneath the monumental tower already alluded to, runs through and communicates with the adjacent main line of railway. From the summit of this tower a very complete view is obtained of the vineyards of the plain, while near its base is the engine-house which supplies the steam for seasoning the newly-made casts that are here steamed, watered, and wined by the thousand. The constant clang of the cooper's hammer and the dull thud of his formidable adze apprise us that the extensive cooperage, which turns out 10,000 casks of all sizes yearly, is close at hand.

The last department of this vast establishment which we visited was the Shipping Bodega, containing a few thousand butts of all the various descriptions of wine ready for shipment. These wines undergo two separate finings, the latter one being of considerable duration. Owing to his large stock Sefior Misa is enabled to fine as many as 1,000 butts of any particular wine that is in demand at the same time. It is his opinion that sherries which have been several months on finings acquire a softness and age which freshly-fined wines never possess. His arrangements in this respect admit of Senor Misa shipping at a moment's notice several hundred butts of wine in perfect condition, as was the case in 1873, when he shipped as many as 1,400 butts during the month of October, believed to be the largest quantity ever shipped by a single house in the same space of time. In the Shipping Bodega samples of wine of the very highest class were offered us to taste, including finos of great character, delicacy, and fragrance, amontillados that had developed their peculiar special qualities in perfection, and olorosos of fine high flavour and aroma.

Another great shipping house is that of Garvey and Co., who can boast of possessing the largest single bodega in Jerez. This vast structure is 600ft. in length by 126ft. in width, and its long vistas of piled-up casks of wine, fading gradually into obscurity, certainly offer an impressive spectacle. By close packing as many as 8,000 butts can be stored beneath this one roof, where a thousand casks of amontillado alone are commonly kept almost ready for shipment.

Although, of course, the firm supplies every class of sherry, amontillado has been its great specialty for upwards of thirty years, when the founder of the house first commenced to ship this wine, unknown up to that period in England. The soleras of amontillado of remarkable age and character stored in this bodega are distinguished by their finesse. At the farther end of an adjacent spacious court are several smaller cellars stored with various kinds of sherry, while an immense number of butts of common wine are stacked beneath the adjoining colonnade. In one of these bodegas, containing only selected soleras, we tasted some wonderfully fine amontillado and a rare old brown sherry the solera of which had been founded by the grandfather of the three brothers who compose the existing firm. When the Prince of Wales was at Jerez in his youthful days he tasted the Garvey wines of that epoch, and gave the palm to this particular specimen, which at that date, I trust, was neither so potent nor so pungent as it is now.

An adjacent five-aisled cellar contains a large stock of young, clean-tasting Montilla wine, which appears to constitute an important feature in the business of the firm, who have an establishment at Lucena, in the heart of the Montilla district, where they make

some 1,500 butts of this wine annually from selected grapes, principally of the Pedro Jimenez variety, purchased of the neighbouring growers. Passing from here through various small courtyards, and glancing at some handsome English mares, the beginning of a breeding-stud, we enter a long narrow cellar where samples of fine Montilla, ranging from eight to twenty-five years old, were submitted to us. All were pale, delicate, and fresh-tasting, while some more matured specimens had acquired that marked etherous flavour and bouquet characteristic of these wines, which assimilate closely to the amontillado type.

Haurie Nephews claim to be the oldest existing firm of shippers of sherry. Its founder was a native of France, and the origin of the house dates back to the early part of the last century. The Haurie of that epoch commenced to ship wine to France from Jerez during the Spanish War of Succession, and when the Peace of Utrecht was signed, hastened to send sherry to England—sherry over which Steele may have become more light-hearted, Swift more morose, Bolingbroke more eloquent, and Addison more didactic. As many as eighteen firms of shippers are said to have sprung from this single house, which plumes itself principally upon its light blended wines of the old-fashioned type, although it has numerous remarkable soleras of amontillado and oloroso, including wines which secured the four first-class medals at the Jerez Exhibition of 1856. The celebrated Breadalbane "stag sherry," which fetched £7 5s. per dozen at the Dalhousie sale last year, was one of the shipments of this notable firm.

The wines we tasted at the Haurie bodegas included a complete scale of amontillados ranging from the mosto of last year up to a wine of about thirty years old. The fine etherous flavour which distinguishes the higher-class amontillados was very apparent in the older samples. Prom about their sixth year the wines grew perceptibly finer with increasing age until we arrived at the upper part of the scale, when their pungency and spirituousness became too pronounced to recommend them for

ordinary consumption. One comparatively youthful sample known as the "Ah!" had a fine fresh fragrant flavour, and while possessing ample body was yet of sufficiently low alcoholic strength to be very agreeable drinking. We subsequently tasted some rich olorosos the pungent flavour of which was subdued by a charming roundness, and finally wound up with a grand blended wine of high but refined flavour and great mellowness, which was priced, as such a wine merited to be, at. £240 a butt.

Don Diego de Agreda has numerous fine soleras of various classes of Jerez wines stored in his bodega, which, divided into as many as eight aisles, communicates with by far the most beautiful garden in all Jerez. Here, even late in the autumn, one found brilliant floral parterres, with choice tropical plants, palms, pines, cedars, cypresses, cacti, orange and pomegranate trees in profusion. Shady elms lined its pleasant walks, swans reflected themselves in its rippling waters, and myriads of goldfish swam in glistening circles around its plashing fountain. Senor de Agreda's house, with its patio in the style of one of the courts of the Alhambra, is no less beautiful than his garden, and his wines are worthy of the taste which these display. His stock numbers between 8,000 and 9,000 butts; and he boasts of some rare old wine purchased five-and-twenty years ago at the rate of.£240 per butt, which had lain in a cellar untouched for more than one generation, and was reputed to be fully a century old. The amontillados we tasted here were perfect, and so were some samples of fino from Senor de Agreda's own vineyard, Las Canas, which produces a remarkably delicate wine.

The establishment of Senor Julian Pemartin—a great sherry shipper, who, finding Jerez had merely a plain-looking Moorish Alcazar, provided it with a highly ornate palace in the Louis Quatorze style—is entered through one of its principal bodegas. Crossing this we find ourselves in a pleasant court planted with trees, and having a picturesque dome-roofed structure in its centre. The old-established house prides itself on its amontillados, several fine samples of which, of gradually-increasing age, we tasted. We were also shown some vino de pasto, a fullflavoured, amber-tinted sherry, of fine quality. The father of Senor Pemartin was the first who introduced a Jerez wine into England under this now well-known but slightly inappropriate name, and his shipments of it met with remarkable success. Samples of wines of the old sherry type, whose tint had deepened with age and not through the medium of vino de color, and some of the soleras of which dated as far back as the year 1818, were next shown to us. Spite of the excessive pungency common to wines of this great age, a real vinous flavour was nevertheless discernible in the majority of them.

The house of Jose Pemartin, owner of the well-known vineyard in the Cerro de Santiago, is an offshoot from the above. Stored in different bodegas are some venerable soleras in casks which have become blackened by age—full-bodied, well-rounded wines, the perfect mellowness of which half a century has not impaired. There, too, we were shown several finely-matured amontillados; also a wine of the old Jerez type, which carried its thirty years buoyantly; and some comparatively juvenile, fresh-tasting, and peculiarly fragrant finos.

Within a stone's throw of the Jerez bull-ring is the spacious bodega of Mr. R. Davies, who has the Torre Breva vineyard at San Lucar, and is proprietor of the celebrated Eibero Seco vineyard, which produces the finest wine in Madeira, where he also owns the villa and gardens of La Vigia, occupied by the Empress of Austria during her residence on that island. Mr. Davies, who takes the lead in the various sports with which the English community settled at Jerez seek to relieve the monotony of an existence sacrificed to the rearing, blending, and shipping of wine for the benefit of their fellow-countrymen, includes in his various stock some fine varieties. At his bodega we tasted a wine known to the *clientele* of the house as la Novia, an excellent amontillado suf-

ficiently old to have developed its finer qualities, and yet light and delicate. We were also shown a beautifully-rounded wine from an ancient solera of Don Miguel Viton's, some remarkably potent rare old wine, and several very delicate finos and manzanillas of different ages from the Torre Breva vineyard, the vintage at which we have described. Mr. J. C. Gordon, like his neighbour Mr. E. Davies, is a wine-grower as well as a shipper. He owns one of the vineyards of the plain which in good years produces 300 butts of wine. At his bodega we met with some fine fragrant olorosos, an old and potent East India brown sherry, and several high-class finos perfectly matured. In this quarter of Jerez the bodega in which Senor J. J. Vegas has recently installed himself is situated. His principal wines are of that type which was in such high favour before the fashion for paler, and too often inferior, varieties set in. The samples we tasted here were from soleras composed of some of the best growths of the Macharnudo and Carrascal districts, rounded by a judicious blending of a small quantity of sweet Pedro Jimenez. These wines, which have very little spirit added to them, ordinarily attain, we were told, in course of years an alcoholic strength of 36 deg. of proof spirit.

On the other side of Jerez and near to the circular line of railway connecting the principal Jerez bodegas are the cellars of Messrs. Wisdom and Warter, who, while shipping sherries of various kinds, make a speciality of wines of the fi.no type, principally from the Montilla district. These wines develop in a limited degree earlier than the Jerez growths, and, while remarkably clean-tasting, exhibited a certain fulness combined with considerable character. As no spirit is added to them until they are on the eve of being shipped, their alcoholic strength in the bodegas is remarkably low. To enable them to travel, however, the older wines have to be brought up to a strength of 32 deg. and the younger ones to 36 deg. With these wines we tasted some choice Montilla of a fabulous age, also a fine fullflavoured wine known in the bodega as "Emperador,"

and several superior samples of sweet Pedro Jimenez.

Near to Messrs. Wisdom and Warter's are the newly-erected bodegas of Mr. R. Ivison, who has numerous fine wines of various types, and especially in the old Jerezano style—wines of remarkable character and not too pungent in flavour. One oloroso, the solera of which dated back to 1846, was exceptionally fine. Mr. Ivison, who is a great partisan of the Seville wines, which are very clean and fresh-tasting, although often of considerable alcoholic strength, hastens the development of certain inferior growths by subjecting them for six months or longer to natural heat under a low galvanised iron roof and in a special bodega admitting of scarcely any ventilation. In the adjoining bodegas of Messrs. Webber and Co. wines of the Jerez fino type are the dominating variety.

Messrs. Mackenzie and Co.'s premises are close to the Jerez railway station, and are entered through a pleasant patio paved with marble and adorned with luxuriant tropical plants. To the left are the offices, to the right the sample-rooms, and beyond are the bodegas, the principal of which, remarkable for its broad aisles, is capable of containing 5,000 butts of-wine, while another couple of thousand can be stored in the smaller cellars and annexes. Here we tasted some fine manzanillas and amontillados, and a very old Jerez wine, the solera of which is said to have been established a century ago. It was of the oloroso type, dark in colour, and without that excessive pungency which these antique wines commonly develop. Far more pungent was an oloroso of greater age, the solera of which is known in the bodegas by the name of "Fernando HI." This wine, we were informed, could not be shipped under. £500 per butt. Another oloroso, valued at £300 per butt, proved to be a fine, deepcoloured, well-rounded wine of great body and character.

Messrs. Heyward and Wilson's bodega, situated in the neighbourhood of the Pemartin Palace, is a handsome, well-lighted structure, with a spiral staircase at one end of it conducting to a platform on the roof, whence a panoramic view of Jerez and its surroundings—including its Alcazar, churches, bodegas, bull-ring, old Moorish towers and battlements, and neighbouring vineyards—is obtained. The wines shipped by this firm are principally Jerez vinos of ordinary and superior quality, manzanillas, and the Montilla growths, with certain robuster varieties of the old Jerezano type.

The ancient convent and church of the Jesuits, closed and sold by order of the State some forty years ago, are to-day the bodegas of Messrs. Matthiesen and Furlong—nave, aisles, choir, and cloisters being alike crowded with butts of sherry ranged as usual in triple tiers. This firm, instead of following the antiquated ways customary in most of the Jerez bodegas, avail themselves of all modern mechanical appliances. In the former refectory of the convent they have a number of large vats, the smallest holding some eight butts, which are used for maturing and fining wines. The most capacious of these vats is reserved for blending purposes, wine being pumped into it from the neighbouring vats through gutta-percha tubing. The court of the cloisters is fitted with apparatus for steaming the new casks, which are here continually revolving in eccentric circles. The house owns a vineyard some considerable distance north-east of Jerez, in the district known as the CuartilloB, which, although not of pure albariza soil, is nevertheless principally chalk, and yields a good type of fino wine. The vines cultivated are the palomino, castellano, and Pedro Jimenez varieties, and the usual annual production amounts to 200 butts. For several years past no yeso has been used in making wine at this vineyard.

To reach Senor Tsasi's bodegas one has to pass through some of the more curious among the old streets of Jerez, where elaborate escutcheons figure above the ornamental doorways of the principal houses, and stone pillars with richly-carved capitals decorate many of their corners. The Tsasi bodegas, being somewhat old-fashioned, are in keeping with these picturesque surroundings, and Senor Ysasi's wines, notably his finos and amontillados, if not of a like remote antiquity, are thoroughly well matured and of high quality.

The bodegas of Messrs. Cramp and Suter are entered through a small but picturesque courtyard roofed in with trellis-work overgrown with vines. On either side are the two principal bodegas with some smaller cellars in their immediate vicinity. The firm have several excellent fino soleras, which, contrary to the general practice, are reared by them in a small and dark bodega; also a few rare old wines, one of which dates back to 1812, the period of the retreat of the French from Moscow, while others scarcely less old had made the voyage to Manilla and back. These wines were highly aromatic, but generally too pungent and too potent for ordinary drinking.

Among the half-dozen establishments of Jerez almacenistas which we visited, the principal and by far the most interesting was that of Senor Sanchez Romate. Here all the wines offered us to taste were of admirable quality, more especially those from high-class vineyards owned by the house, among which are La Soledad, some 110 acres in extent, and Los Quadrados, both in the Balbaina district, with the vineyards of La Carrina in the Macharnudo and San Bias in the Carrascal districts. The sample from La Carrina, which had passed through three criaderas during the first four years of its youth, and had afterwards been on a solera for a period of eight years, was of excellent quality, still the wine which especially commended itself to our taste was a splendid fino, some ten years old, from the Santa Cecilia vineyard, and which to great freshness and softness of flavour and remarkable strength united a most captivating fragrance. Among the more curious wines were some very old Jerczano of singular mellowness from a solera established by Don Juan Sanchez about a century ago, a venerable and highly-concentrated moscatel which had more of the character of a liqueur than a wine, a delicate and rare wine the produce of

the small moscatel grape from the Soledad vineyard, and several finos, amontillados, and pasados of very refined flavour, the soleras of which were stored in the Bodega del-huerta, one of the old Moorish towers which rise at intervals above the battlemented walls on this side of Jerez.

IX.—The Wines Of The Bay Of Cadiz, Chiclana, And Teebujena.

The Vineyards of Puerto Real and Puerto de Santa Maria—A Rival to the Great Sherry Metropolis—Evidences of Decadence—Duff Gordon and Co.'s Establishment, Garden Court, and Rare Soleras—The Bodegas of Sefior M. de Mora, Superior Finos, Moscatcl, Pedro Jimenez, and Jerezano Wine —Cosens and Co.'s Bodegas and High-class Soleras of Manzanillas, Fiuos, and Amontillados—The Gonzalez Bodegas in an Abandoned Convent—The Admirable Wines of Sefior Gastelu—The Choice Finos and Amontillados of Mr. J. W. Burdon—Rota, its Vineyards, Market-gardens, and Moorish Remains—Interior of a Rota Wine-produciug Establishment—Mode of Making the Sacramental Tent—Chipiona and its Vineyards—The Road to Chiclana—Chiclana famous alike for its Bull-fighters and its Wines— Trebujena.

In addition to the many thousand acres of vineyards at Jerez and San Lucar, producing almost all the finer wines, there are others which belong to the sherry district proper. The towns and villages claiming a Phoenician origin that dot the shores of the beautiful Bay of Cadiz are all more or less noted for their wines. The manzanilla of San Lucar, and the tintilla or so-called tent of Rota, are widely known in England, but the other wines enjoy merely a local renown, and are commonly either mingled with those of Jerez or else boldly shipped as Jerez growths. Puerto Real, lying equidistant between Jerez and Cadiz, has only a few vineyards, which being in the lowlands their produce, both as regards quantity and quality, is of no great account. It is different, however, with Puerto de Santa Maria, the vineyards of which are not only extensive, but adjoin those of Jerez on their eastern side. The Puerto, moreover, ships no less than 20,000 butts of wine annually, or considerably more than its total production, much of which, by the way, goes to Jerez; consequently it has to draw a certain proportion of the wine it ships from other districts, including even Jerez itself.

Puerto de Santa Maria is in fact a Jerez on a smaller scale, and, so far as wine is concerned, a kind of rival to the great sherry metropolis, just as centuries ago it was more than the rival of Cadiz as a port. The palaces raised by its merchant princes of bygone times, and to-day converted to ignoble uses, are in a sadly dilapidated condition. Their richly-carved doorways are crumbling away; their proud scutcheons are well-nigh obliterated; their marble patios — those elegant arcaded courts of Moorish origin and design with sculptured fountains in the centre—are going rapidly to ruin. An occasional small passenger steamer, some scores of fishing boats, and a few lighters are the only craft that now enter the ample harbour of Puerto de Santa Maria, which a still-existing Moorish castle once defended. Indeed, the Puerto does not even ship its own wine direct, but sends it in barges to the Trocadero mole, some four or five miles distant.

The wines of the Puerto are in every respect the counterpart of those of Jerez, excepting that they are, in a measure, inferior to the finer varieties of the more renowned viticulture! district, owing to the best soils being of scarcely the same favourable character. Generally speaking, they are from the same species of grape, are made in exactly the same manner, while their aftertreatment is in all respects precisely similar. Indeed, the most experienced judge would tail to detect any difference between the ordinary produce of the respective districts. The oldest shipping house at the Puerto de Santa Maria is the well-known one of Duff Gordon and Co., whose bodegas are reached through a charming garden court, bordered with handsome flowering shrubs and with clusters of fine old trees towering in the centre. Geraniums in all their splendour,

with ivy and other climbing plants, are trained up the walls, hiding all but the entrances to the cellars. Of these the spacious shipping bodega, remarkable for its wide passages between the several rows of casks—all posed in perfectly straight lines, and exactly level one with another—contains 3,000 butts of various kinds of sherry wine. Four other bodegas are devoted to soleras comprising some singularly delicate finos ten years old, with amontillados of decided yet refined flavour, and olorosos of subdued pungent taste and rich aroma. For one of these last-named wines.£400 per butt had been offered and refused, it being considered much too valuable for blending purposes to be parted with even at this price. Over the door of the Duff Gordon sample-room projects the stuffed head of a wild-looking short-horned bull, which at some corrida de toros at the Puerto had killed its eleven horses and remained the master of the ring.

Another important shipping house is that of Sefior M. de Mora, whose stock of wine exceeds 10,000 butts. All the appointments of this great establishment, which is also set off with its floral parterres and rows of orange-trees, are of the most perfect kind. Machinery has been brought into requisition, not only for steaming and washing, but for gauging and even moistening the outsides of empty casks, so as to prevent tbe staves from shrinking. In the bodegas, too, the lower butts are supported on light iron stands instead of the usual cumbersome wooden beams or blocks of stone. Travelling stages are, moreover, provided to enable the wine to be drawn from the upper casks without the men having to climb up from one butt to the other according to the prevailing practice. At these bodegas we tasted some finos with a delicate bouquet and soft aromatic flavour; a full, luscious, and powerfully-perfumed moscatel, priced at.£300 the butt; a spirituous Pedro Jimenez of the consistency of syrup, and some rich amber-tinted Jerezano wine of great age but remarkably refined flavour.

Messrs. Cosens and Co., of Jerez, have several large bodegas at Puerto de

Santa Maria. The court of their principal premises here is planted with flower-beds, orange, cypress, mulberry, and flowering laurel-trees, rising among which are a profusion of casks and piles of oak staves, as though every square foot of vacant ground had to be turned to some useful purpose. In the remarkably cool bodega where the firm keep some of their highclass soleras are manzanillas of fine fresh aromatic flavour and powerful floral bouquet, Jerez finos, cool to the palate, and with that tender almond taste which recalls the rarer growths of the Rheingau, and amontillados that are almost essences while still continuing to be wines. Messrs. Gonzalez and Co. haTe also their bodegas at the Puerto, an abandoned convent being crowded with wines of theirs, comprising exclusively the cheaper qualities. The bodegas of Senores Gastelu contain 4,000 butts of exclusively high-class wines, principally choice finos with remarkably fragrant bouquets and of varied degrees of delicate yet sufficiently pronounced flavour, together with some highly odorous, matured, well-rounded amontillados. Each of these admirable wines seemed to have a distinct character of its own. At the bodega of Mr. J. W. Burdon we also met with some exquisite finos of great fragrance and delicacy, and went through an interesting scale of amontillados of splendid quality.

Rota lies to the north-west of Puerto de Santa Maria, and close to the seashore. The road for some little distance is bordered by acacia-trees, a perfect novelty in the sherry district, for leave Jerez on whichever side you will not a single tree along the public highway will obstruct your view. Trees, say the Jerez agriculturists, harbour birds, and birds only devour our crops, therefore we keep our fields and highways completely clear of trees. After the last tree in the outskirts of the Puerto is passed the road skirts numerous patches of vines, planted in either loamy or sandy soils, known respectively as barros and arenas. It then intersects a broad plain, dotted over with white casas and cortijos, with their adjacent cattle-sheds and huge stacks of straw, and bounded on the left by a range of heights laid out as olive groves and pine plantations. Ahead there rises up a steep hill overgrown with vines, and having at its summit an ancient telegraph tower. Some little distance farther on the road to Rota branches off to the left, and we ascend a gentle slope crowned by a dark pine wood, and soon the bright blue sea and low Moorish-looking houses of Rota appear in sight. Vineyards are here intermingled with tomato fields, and market gardens furnished with the old-fashioned Moorish norias, with their revolving wheels and earthenware jars, by means of which the land is irrigated. Rota contributes largely to the supply of not merely Puerto de Santa Maria, but also of Jerez and Cadiz, with fruit and vegetables. Of this we soon have evidence in the troops of mules and donkeys which we meet laden with their canastos of tomatoes, sweet capsicums, ruddy pomegranates, young green peas, and spring radishes as large as ordinary carrots.

The first view of Rota is somewhat picturesque. To the right is an abandoned bodega and an ancient mansion with an elaborate escutcheon above its richly-ornate doorway. To the left is a quaint little chapel standing among weeping willows and cypresses, while iu front the ill-paved calle principal of the little seaside town presents a long vista of one-storied, whitewalled houses with the conventional barred windows, and gargoyles projecting from their low and occasionally overhanging roofs, along which rows of pumpkins are laid to dry. Rota boasts the remnants of some Moorish ramparts which defended it on the side facing the sea, and a fine old Moorish castle with wellpreserved battlements and towers; also a remarkably curious church, originally a mosque, with an elaborately-sculptured choir worthy of any cathedral; and some handsome chapels, the walls and dome of one of which are covered with painted tiles of singularly fantastic design.

On visiting one of the largest wine-producing establishments, an almost windowless house, with a massive square tower in the Moorish style, one observed the customary lagares ranged under a low arcade, with the usual well in the centre of the court, and piles of dried grape-skins heaped up around. Near the lagares stood an antique-looking screw-press, used in the making of the tintilla—the well-known sacramental Tent—for which Rota is so celebrated. The grapes, a small dark red variety, after being exposed to the sun for eight days, are passed through a sieve to separate them from their stalks. They are afterwards thrown into a large butt stood on end, and when this is almost three-parts full six arrobas or twenty-one gallons of vino de color are added to them. A man now gets carefully into the cask, which by this time is very nearly full, and turns over the grapes with his hands and stirs them about with his feet as well as with a wooden shovel; the result being that they are partially crushed and thoroughly saturated with the vino de color. The mixture is left in the same casks for six weeks or longer, during which time it ferments and acquires great depth of colour from the skins of the grapes. The latter are now emptied out and placed under the press on mats of esparto, and, the final juice having been extracted and mixed with that which has already flowed from the fruit, the must is poured into other butts.

A common red wine is made at Rota somewhat after the same system as is pursued with respect to the tintilla, the main difference being that ordinary white wine is used instead of vino de color. About a thousand butts of white wine are vintaged annually at Rota from the same species of grapes, but according to the process of vinification prevalent in the other sherry districts. The Alcalde of Rota, whom we found sitting in a little wine-shop kept by his son and surrounded by a veritable court of muleteers, waggoners, and market-gardeners, informed us that there were some 2,200 acres of vineyards in the Rota district, more than one-fourth of which are the property of the Duc de Montpensier. They produce a considerable quantity of grapes for table purposes in addition to 1,400 butts of wine, not more than 120 of which, however, are tintilla of Rota, or sacramental Tent.

Chipiona, picturesquely situated a few miles farther along the shores of the Bay of Cadiz, amid the same remnants of Moorish battlements and towers as characterise all the towns and villages hereabouts, produces a few hundred butts of white wine annually, all of which find their way either to Jerez or San Lucar. It is, however, more especially noted for its splendid moscatel grapes, which are grown on the sand so close to the seashore that every patch of half-a-dozen vines has to be surrounded by its dwarf fence to prevent the wind from the sea blowing away the soil and leaving the roots of the vines bare.

The wine-producing district of Chiclana lies on the other side of Cadiz, and is reached from Jerez by railway to San Fernando, and thence by a few miles' cut across the surrounding salt marshes. At the time of our visit, late in the autumn, the journey was a pleasant one, for some heavy showers had sensibly moderated the heat, although the sun was still sufficiently powerful and the sky of as deep a blue as ever. Autumn and spring appear to combine at this particular season in Andalusia, for while flowering chrysanthemums and ripe pomegranates abounded in all the gardens barley was sprouting in the fields and olive groves, purple primroses were blooming by the sandy roadside, and fresh green peas were coming daily to market. On leaving Jerez the railway runs for a short distance past vineyards and isolated olive groves, with the Guadalete winding through the adjacent marshy plain, and the small castle, replacing the one where unhappy Dona Blanca was confined by Peter the Cruel, crowning a jutting ridge on our right hand. Next come the works for supplying Cadiz with fresh water, by means of a reservoir half-way up a lofty hill, at the foot of which are some extensive stone quarries, where in the spring of this year a youth sequestrated from his family at Algar, some thirty miles distant, was secreted until the stipulated ransom was paid to his brigand captors. After crossing the Guadalete at Puerto de Santa Maria the line runs through salt marshes and moorland, past huge white pyramids of salt and dark green pine woods, skirting on the one hand the plain where Roderick, last ruler of the Goths in Spain, risked the decisive battle which lost him his kingdom and his life, and with the white walls and towers of Cadiz rising, as it were, from out the deep blue sea on the other.

From San Fernando to Chiclana was little more than halfan-hour's drive, the four horses of our carretela being incited by coaxings, scoldings, and judicious applications of the whip to gallop all the way. The route lies first across an old fortified stone bridge on the outskirts, then over a bridge of boats, and finally between two long canals communicating with the neighbouring saltworks which extend for a considerable distance around. A gloomy pine wood, stretching for miles inland, skirts o S the road on the left just before we reach Chiclana, which, intersected by the little river Lirio, lies on the slope of a steep hul. Chiclana is equally noted for its bull-fighters as for its-wines, having given birth to more celebrated toreadores than any other town in Spain, notably those famous rival matadors, Francisco Montes and Jose Bedondo— better known as el Chiclanero— with whose exploits all Spain rang during the early years of the reign of the ex-Queen Isabella. Not merely the cities but all the towns hereabouts have their bull-rings, where spavined horses are annually gored by hundreds, and bulls slaughtered in scores, amidst frantic exclamations of delight on the part of the sanguinary audiences which these sickening spectacles never fail to attract. On the other side of tho hill, crowned by a little chapel on the site of a former hermitage, are the Chiclana vineyards, producing in favourable years about 4,000 butts of passably good wine, which finds its principal market at Jerez, where it is mixed with the ordinary Jerez growths. The few samples we tasted were all fresh in flavour and possessed considerable body, and, although invariably young, seemed as if they would develop a certain amount of char-

acter.

One other insignificantwine-producing locality completes what may be regarded as the real sherry district. This is Trebujena, a neglected, shabby-looking little town perched on the summit *of* a hill some fifteen miles due north of Jerez, and shut out in a measure from all intercourse with surrounding localities. To reach it one has to cross a vast uncultivated plain called the Llanos of Caulina, at one end of which the Jerez racecourse and cricket-ground are situated, whilst crowning a little hillock at the other are the ruins of the Moorish castle of Melgarejo. The quantity of wine vintaged at Trebujena is comparatively small, and its quality is of no marked character.

X.—Wines Of The Seville And Mooter Districts.

Seville and the Gipsy Suburb of Triana—Vineyards on the High Lands near the Guadalquivir — The House where Cortes died — The Wine-producing districts of Gines, Villanueva, Espartina, and Salterns—System of Vinification—Price of Grapes and Mosto—The Vineyards of San Lucar la Mayor and Manzanilla—The fresh-tasting Ambrosial Wine of the latter— The Condado de Niebla and its Low-Class Wines—The Vintage in the Moguer district — The Wines shipped as Sherry — Moguer the Port Columbus sailed from.

Few sherry-drinkers are aware that the shippers of this popular wine derive a certain portion of their supply from districts not merely scores but even hundreds of miles away from the true sherry region, which in reality only extends from twelve to sixteen miles around Jerez. In the first place, the whole of that tract of undulating country which stretches from Seville—noted rather for its olives and its oranges than its wines—to Huelva on the extreme south-west coast of Spain, has numerous vineyards interspersed among its miles upon miles of olive groves, and produces wines of variable although rarely high quality, most of which are exported, blended with Jerez growths, as sherry. To reach this viticultural re-

gion we proceeded along the valley of the Guadalquivir as far as Seville, the most fascinating of Andalusian cities; the ancient Phoenician settlement of whose conquest in after times Ceesar was so proud; the early capital of the Gothic kings; the city which still bears such striking traces of Soman, Moorish, and mediaeval splendour; the port whence CortiSs and Pizarro sailed to the conquest of Mexico and Peru; and the birthplace of the two greatest painters that Spain has produced—Bartolome Esteban Murillo and Velasquez de Silva.

The nearest vineyards are all on the high lands on the opposite side of the Guadalquivir to that on which Seville stands, and a few miles beyond the gipsy suburb of Triana, where John Philip had his studio and found the subjects for so many of his pictures of Andalusian life. After crossing the flat and uninteresting plain which borders the Moors famous " river of delight," the road, skirted by trees and aloes and bustling with country carts and mules laden with firewood, winds round one of a series of bold, cultivated hills, where in the month of November beans and barley were sprouting up around-the gnarled grey trunks of thousands upon thousands of ancient olive-trees. The first vineyards are sighted just before we reach the summit of the hill after passing through Castilleja de la Cuesta, where a bronze bust and a gilt tablet over a restored antique doorway in the village high street indicate the house where the truculent conqueror of Mexico died in disgrace and indigence. Some little distance to the right, and encompassed by plantations of vines and olives, is the straggling village *of* Gines. Here, as soon as it was known that we had been inquiring for el Senor Alcalde, symptoms of disquiet at once manifested themselves, for it was thought we were Government functionaries connected with the detested conscription. The alcalde, who was discussing with the baker the regulation price of bread as our vehicle came to a halt in front of the village ayuntamiento, informed us that Gines had only between one and two hundred acres of vineyards, all planted principally with the garrido species of grape, and yielding ordinarily 400 butts of white wine, valued at the time of being drawn off the lees at from £4 10s. to £6 per butt when taken from the bodega.

We found that this price only slightly varied at other places in the neighbourhood—notably Villanueva, Espartina, and Salteras—having among them a couple of thousand acres of vineyards interspersed between vast tracts of olive grounds, and producing in favourable years some 10,000 butts of wine, instead of the third of that quantity, which resulted from the vintage just concluded. The prevailing soil in which the vines are planted is reddish clay, indicative of the presence of oxide of iron, while the subsoil is chalk, and hence a certain character in the better-class growths of this locality. The vintage in the neighbourhood of Seville ordinarily commences about the middle of September, and is conducted much the same as throughout the Jerez district, the only difference being a slight variation in the mode of crushing the grapes. There are no means of pressing these in the vineyards, the lagares and presses being invariably adjacent to the bodegas in the different villages. After having been trodden in capacious stone lagares on a level with the floor of the presshouse, the grapes are piled up in a broad heap and bound round with long bands of esparto, a cumbersome screw-press with a huge heavy beam, some twenty feet long and four feet in diameter, being employed to extract the remaining juice. The vintagers are paid at the rate of seven to eight reals (18d. to 20d.) per day, and, as at Jerez, are invariably of the male sex, women in Spain never being allowed to take part in the vintage, although they assist largely at the subsequent olive harvest.

Grapes had been sold, we found, in the Seville district at from 3 to 4 reals, or 7d. to 10d., the arroba of 25£lbs. The answers we received to numerous inquiries as to the quantity of yeso used in making the Seville wines agreed in stating that this amounted to *41* lbs. to each

butt of mosto. Generally this mosto is drawn off the lees by the purchaser, who in a majority of instances adds a small percentage of spirit to it. When, however, it is drawn off by the grower, spirit is only added in the event of the wine getting out of order. At different bodegas we tasted several young unripe wines and also wines ranging from five to six years old. The latter had an agreeable bouquet, and were of a soft, light, pleasant flavour, which we found became much more spirituous in wines of greater age. These so-called Seville wines are scarcely consumed at all on the spot; they are, however, commonly drunk at Seville itself, and considerable quantities of them are purchased by the Jerez shippers mainly to serve as the basis for cheap sherries. Messrs. Gonzalez and Co. have a large bodega at Seville, which, like other establishments of the same nature, was formerly an abandoned convent; and here they store a large stock of the better class of Seville wines.

San Lucar la Mayor, some eight miles from Salteras, like all the towns and villages hereabouts, is perched on the summit of a hill, and surrounded by olive-groves, orchards, and vineyards. Its wine is of no particular repute, but it is very different with that of Manzanilla, some fourteen miles farther along the high road from Seville to Huelva. The Manzanilla vineyards produce a wine bearing so striking a resemblance to the celebrated growths of San Lucar de Barrameda, that these latter have come to be universally known under the same name. The slopes of the hill on which Manzanilla is situated are covered with vines, and all the well-to-do inhabitants of the place have their bodegas stocked with the fresh-tasting ambrosial wine of which the little village is so justly proud.

Manzanilla is the last wine-growing locality along our route that produces wine of any character; an extensive viticultural district known as the Condado de Niebla yields, however, a considerable quantity of low-class sweetish white wine, nearly the whole of which finds its way to Moguer, a little town

on the Rio Tinto, where of late years a brisk trade in wine has been carried on. The vintage hereabouts takes place in the middle of September, the different species of grapes cultivated in the district, including the garrido macho and fino, palomino, mantuo, perruano, zalema, and the mantuo de San Lucar, being all mingled in the lagares, and the coarser stalks even not being removed. Prior to our visit, at the opening of the vintage, grapes in the Moguer district were sold for as little as two reals, or fivepence, the arroba of 25£lbs.; but when the extent of the expected falling off in the Jerez crop became known, the price gradually rose until it had doubled itself. The pressing of the grapes is accomplished in the same fashion as prevails in the neighbourhood of Seville, and when the mosto is drawn off the lees in the spring somewhat less than 1 per cent. of spirit is added to it. Should the wine remain for a second year in the grower's hands this is ordinarily supplemented at the end of that time by a similar quantity of alcohol. The commonest wines are converted into spirit, an operation which manages to keep a couple of distilleries at Moguer constantly at work.

The Jerez shippers are somewhat reticent as to the extent to which they avail themselves of the Moguer growths, and affect to speak contemptuously of these wines. It is, nevertheless, quite certain that some 15,000 butts of the wines in question are sent away from Moguer regularly every year, the bulk being no doubt shipped to England as sherry, principally from the Trocadero mole, and to some extent even from Moguer itself, the port whence four centuries ago Columbus sailed with his little fleet on that famous first transatlantic voyage which resulted in the discovery of the West Indies. On the summit of a height rising from the seashore some few miles distant stands the abandoned convent of La Babida, where Columbus sought shelter, and so impressed the prior with the truth of his theories that the latter accorded him a steady protection, which led eventually to the realisation of the adventurous navigator's longcherished projects.

XL—The Montilla Wines.—Concluding Remabks.

The Town of Montilla encircled by Sierras—The Birthplace of el Grand Capitan Oonzalo of Cordova—The Castillo and Palacio of the Dukes of Medina-Celi—The ancient Ducal Bodega of La Tercia—Its Centenarian Casks and Grand Solera—The Teatro and Tres Naves Bodegas—The Presshonse, its antiquated Press and huge Tinajas—Vineyards of the Sierra de Montilla and the Moriles District—System of Vinification—Fermentation of the Mosto in the Tinajas—Removal of the Wine in Goatskins—Vineyard Value and Price of Grapes—The Wine-growing Districts of AguDar, Monturque, Cabra, and Lucena—Concluding Remarks upon Sherry in general.

Moee than a hundred miles eastward of Seville, and in the famous province of Cordova, is the well-known wine-growing district of Montilla, one of the numerous appanages of the grand dukedom of Medina-Celi. Montilla, walled and fortified in olden times like all the surrounding towns, stands, like them, on the crest of a steep hill encircled on all sides by distant sierras. The castillo is at the eastern extremity of the town, and to reach it you climb the narrow, winding, precipitous, ill-paved streets leading up to the principal church, passing on the way the humble white-walled little house where the great ancestor of the Dukes of Medina-Celi—el gran capitan Gonzalo of C6rdova—was born. From the terraced courtyard in front of the castillo a splendid view is obtained over the surrounding vineyards and forests of olive-trees, so symmetrically planted that when viewed from a height they present a perfect diaper pattern, regular as the squares upon a chessboard. The castillo itself—a building erected at different periods—is flanked by a couple of battlemented towers, while the large hall which forms the principal portion of the edifice has been converted into a bodega. The Dukes of Medina-Celi never resided at the castillo, but at the so-called palacio, a singularly plain but roomy edifice facing

a large square on the other side of the town, and in close proximity to the unpretentious little alameda where the Montillanos are accustomed to assemble on summer evenings.

The ancient ducal bodegas, with all their grand soleras, passed some years ago into the possession of Messrs. Gonzalez, who are to-day holders of the finest Montilla wines in the country, several of them being, in fact, unique. The principal bodega, erected at the commencement of the last century, at a period when the dukes used to receive their rents in kind, still bears the name of La Tercia, from the circumstance that here one-third of the produce of the land used to be handed over by the cultivator as the landlord's share. The Medina-Celi bodegas are situated in the market-place of Montilla, which was crowded at the time of our visit with singularly picturesque groups, the women in light-coloured shawls and fichus, the men in the orthodox turban hats, and wrapped up in capacious cloaks with innumerable folds, their trousers slit half-way to the knee, and their leathern gaiters unlaced, so as to display the clean white stocking beneath. The arriving and departing mules exhibited the customary redundance of ragged trappings. On the opposite side of the market-place rose a group of quaint Spanish houses, flanked by the cold grey walls of some abandoned convent, forming an appropriate background to the animated scene.

An old archway, above which is carved the shield of the Medina-Celis, with its many proud quarterings, leads into the paved courtyard of La Tercia, planted round with orange-trees, and having vines trained up the low white-walled buildings surrounding it. To the left is the low doorway of the ancient bodega, where casks nearly a couple of centuries old are ranged in two tiers on a venerable framework of massive oak. There is a strange antiquated air about the whole place, which is but dimly lighted by a single small window. Huge spiders have spun gigantic webs from butt to butt, or between the blackened beams of the slanting roof. The centenarian casks are of a dull greenish hue,

and their thin iron hoops are so corroded that it is a miracle how the very slim staves manage to hold together. These casks were evidently the work of coopers ignorant of how more substantial staves than those here employed could be bent into shape.

The grand solera stored in this bodega is believed to have been founded prior to the erection of the bodega itself. It comprises as many as eight ascending scales, the youngest wine of which under ordinary circumstances would rank as old. To replenish this solera, wines of the first quality have to be procured from time to time, and nursed for years. We tasted numerous samples of the result, and were struck with the varieties of flavour and bouquet apparent even in different butts belonging to the same scale. One had a soft ambrosial taste, while some possessed the raciness and freshness of flavour of a grand Rhine wine. Others had a rich nutty taste and smell, while others were delicately aromatic. As the samples grew older they deepened in colour and exhibited a refined etherous flavour and odour, which eventually became so powerful as to render the most ancient among them far from agreeable drinking.

Two other bodegas, known respectively as the Teatro and Tres Naves, contain Montilla wines somewhat less delicate in character, but of a fine oloroso type, the produce of the celebrated Moriles district. Adjoining is the press-house, with its antiquated heavy beam-presses, while on either side of the entrance gateway are the huge tinajas, or capacious earthenware jars, sunk deep into the earth, and used for fermenting the wine. In one corner of the plaza facing the palacio Messrs. Gonzalez and Co. have a distillery, where they produce spirit from sound Montilla wines purchased for the special purpose.

The finer Montilla growths come exclusively from the Sierra de Montilla, and the district of Moriles lying on the other side of the range of hills on which the neighbouring fortified towns of Aguilar and Monturque are perched. No regular roads conduct to them, and it is necessary to make the excursion on horseback along such caminos de herraduras as wind round the sides of the mountain. For a certain portion of the way we followed the high road, with olive-groves, vineyards, and highlycultivated fields on either side; but after a few miles we branched off, and soon commenced a toilsome ascent of slopes becoming gradually steeper and steeper, but over-which the plough had nevertheless recently passed, leaving no track whatever for us to follow. The vines were merely so many gnarled and blackened stumps, having already undergone their autumnal pruning, while many had trenches round them to receive the autumn rains. The finer soils are albariza, though not of the same extreme whiteness as in the Jerez district. Two species of vines predominate—the Pedro Jimenez and the baladi, the former being much more prevalent than the latter. All the finer vineyards have their casus with the requisite conveniences for pressing the grapes, the same as the vineyards around Jerez. The old cumbersome beam-press, however, is almost universally used. The system of vinification in the Montilla district is as follows:—The Pedro Jimenez grapes, which ripen the earliest, are gathered from two to three weeks before the others, and carried in tall vase-shaped baskets called cestos, each holding upwards of 60 lbs., to the stone lagares, where they are trodden and pressed, usually without any admixture of gypsum. The pressing finished, the mosto is emptied into those vast earthenware jars called tinajas of which we have already spoken—the largest of which will hold nearly 400 gallons of mosto. When these jars— which are sunk some five feet into the ground, and provided with steps to enable the men to fill and empty them conveniently— are about two-thirds full, the mosto is left to ferment, the mouth of the jar remaining uncovered while fermentation is going on. In a fortnight or three weeks' time the jars are filled up with the must resulting from the pressure of the baladi grapes— a coarser species ripening later than the Pedro Jimenez. A second fermentation

of course follows, and when its more violent character has subsided the mouths of the jars are covered with wooden lids, and the mosto is left until the early spring. On being removed from the jars it is placed in pallejos—i.e., thoroughly-seasoned goatskins—or else in small casks, both of which are slung across the backs of mules, and in this way the wine is conveyed to the Montilla bodegas, where it is at once emptied into ordinary casks. The vintagers receive 5 reals or a trifle over a shilling a day, while the men employed at the presses get half as much again. The value of an acre of vineyard of albariza soil in the Moriles district is £60; vineyards less favourably situated being worth about one-third of that amount and upwards per acre. In the best vineyards only a single butt of wine per acre is calculated upon, whereas the commoner soils will readily yield a couple of butts. The finer grapes are not sold by the growers, but are made by them into wine; inferior grapes, however, can be bought in any quantity at the rate of 25 lbs. for 10d. The latter are pressed at the bodegas in the town, and much of the wine yielded by them goes to Malaga, whereas all the finest Montilla finds its way to Jerez. The wine is preferred by certain shippers there because it enjoys the reputation of ripening a couple of years earlier than the Jerez growths.

In the neighbourhood of Montilla there are other considerable wine-growing districts whose produce is in some repute, although it falls far short of first-class Montilla. These are Aguilar, Monturque, Cabra, and Lucena, the latter being by far the most important. It is here, by the way, that those capacious earthenware jars called tinajas are made.

These pages may be fitly closed with a few remarks, the result of a lengthened study under especially favourable circumstances of numerous wines, produced not only from very different Boils, but from widely different species of grapes; and all of which are shipped to England under the generic name of sherry. I have already shown that the small quantity of gypsum used in making these wines is productive of no

harmful result. That it converts certain tartrates into sulphates is true enough; but if any one imagines that it does this to the extent of changing the flavour of the wine in the smallest degree, or that sherry, fermented without having had gypsum added to it, possesses any of that fresh acidulous flavour which sound judges so much admire in wines of more northern latitudes, he is greatly mistaken. I have frequently compared wines from the same vineyard made with and without gypsum, and have been unable to detect the slightest indication of any more acid flavour in the latter than in the former. At San Lucar the grapes are gathered earlier than at Jerez, and consequently not quite so ripe. This has the effect of imparting to young manzanilla a certain freshness of flavour,-which is, however, equally apparent in wines made with or without gypsum. With regard to the sulphuring which sherry is said to undergo, I am able to assert that the practice has almost ceased at Jerez, where the shippers as a rule decline all offers of wines that have been sulphured.

I have come to the conclusion that it is impossible to have sherry good and at the same time cheap. Even the commonest growths require to be kept for three or four years before they are suitable for drinking, and the nursing of sherry in a bodega for four years simply means doubling its original cost. The wine in its youth is liable to constant perturbation, and under such conditions is of course a most unwholesome beverage.

Disturbing it in any way, sending it jolting upon bullock-carts from one bodega to another, subjecting it to the motion it must necessarily encounter during a sea voyage, and exposing it to great changes of temperature—all of these things tend to revive a fermentation that has not thoroughly completed itself. My own opinion is that there is something radically wrong in the mode of fermenting wines in the south of Spain. It takes place,

I believe, at too high a temperature, in vessels too small for the purpose, with the must not sufficiently exposed to the action of the atmosphere, and subjected, moreover, to frequent great changes of temperature and other disturbing influences. If properly fermented in the first instance, so fine and robust a wine as a first-class Jerez growth—the produce of a magnificent grape, grown in an exceptionally suitable soil, under the most favourable climatic influences—ought not to require spirit added to it to enable it to travel even during the years of its youth.

A cheap sherry, no matter the district whence it comes, whether from Moguer, Seville, or even La Mancha— for certain shippers go as far afield as the country of Don Quixote for their _wine—must necessarily be a young, undeveloped wine / liable to get out of order tlie moment it is moved. As it is originally of a pale dull colour, vino de color has to be added to give it a marketable tint. Some dulce, moreover, is requisite to round off its rawness, which of itself is sufficient to revive fermentation, and, as a consequence, spirit has to be added in considerable quantities to render the wine what is termed "safe." Our wine-merchants are mainly responsible for any excess of added spirit to the higher-class sherries. Over and over again we were told that they positively demand it of the shipper, who, if left to himself and not made responsible, as he most absurdly is, for the condition of the wine for two years after it leaves his possession, would send it over containing several degrees less of spirit. It is excess of added spirit, and not gypsum or sulphur, which is the real bane of sherry.

If, instead of wines being shipped when they are merely a year old, they were kept for another three years, and the absurd practice of fining them, which simply emasculates them, were dispensed with, they might be shipped with a very slight addition of spirit— scarcely more than one-sixth of the quantity they receive at present. In this case we should have a tolerably developed wine, with a decided vinous flavour, unmasked by added alcohol, and consequently without that fieriness common to the cheap sherries we get at present. To please the public eye a trifle of vino de color might be necessary, but this would be in no way detrimental. A fair wine of the above character could, however, scarcely be shipped under.£22 per butt; whereas so keen is competition, that shipments of new wines are made at present at as low a rate as from. £12 to £14.

In my judgment the quality of the finer Jerez wines, and particularly of the high-class ones, is materially impaired by the fining which these undergo, in obedience to public caprice, with the view of insuring an excessive brightness prior to shipment. This is more especially the case with finos, which lose much of their characteristic yet refined flavour and more of their bouquet by the process. In the bodega of Mr. J. W. Burdon at Puerto de Santa Maria, I had the opportunity of comparing some admirable finos with the same wines fined for shipment, and in every instance the latter had perceptibly suffered both in flavour and perfume. Indeed, after added spirit, this practice of fining is the next thing that tends to deteriorate the higher qualities of sherry.

Wines of the amontillado and oloroso character improve materially by being kept from two to five years, and even longer, in bottle. They become softer and rounder, losing much of that high, pungent flavour which they acquire with increasing age. On the other hand, wines of the fino type which have not been saturated with spirit, not merely do not improve but positively deteriorate after having been in bottle for a twelve-month. The so-called bottle flavour, in fact, simply destroys their ambrosial freshness, and impairs alike their elegance and their delicacy.

The question of admitting wine containing more than theregulation 26 of proof spirit at the lowest rate of duty— namely, Is. per gallon—is again undergoing discussion, and certainly the growers of sherry are justified in their protests. For so far as my own researches enable me to judge, it is beyond question— spite of the investigations made some years ago by the agents of Her Majesty's Customs—that sherry as its age increases will develop a higher strength than 26 degrees when not even a drain of extraneous spirit has been added to it from the moment the grapes were pressed in the lagar. This is doubtless due to the evaporation of the aqueous portion of the wine in the hot and dry climate of Jerez, and which is estimated by the rearers of sherry at 4 per cent. and upwards annually. In the Jerez bodegas I constantly came across wine of the very highest character, to which, according to reliable evidence, no more than 1 per cent. of spirit had been added, and yet by the time it was twenty years old—no exceptional age, it must be remembered, for a Jerez wine—it indicated from 33 to 34 of proof spirit.

Sherry-growers say with justice that in the face of these facts it is unfair to place Spanish wines, or the wines of southern latitudes generally, on the same basis as the wines of France and Germany, which naturally are much below the former in alcoholic strength; and this more especially since the British Customs have virtually surrendered their theory that it is impossible for any natural wine to develop more than the orthodox 26 degrees. The tests, made under the authority of this department, of natural wines sent to the International Exhibition of 1874 showed in fact that, in addition to Spanish wines, admittedly pure samples of the wines of Australia, Greece, and Portugal contained 30.3 to 28.4 and 31.2 degrees of proof spirit respectively. With such. results as these the existing limit of the shilling duty can scarce;, be maintained.

CPSIA information can be obtained at www.ICGtesting.com
Printed in the USA
LVOW05s1934280514

387630LV00018B/902/P

9 781230 344041